F. Iunipero Serra

A BICENTENNIAL MEMOIR

A Bicentennial Compendium of
Maynard J. Geiger's

The Life And Times Of

by
Msgr. Francis J. Weber
1988

*This book bears the official
endorsement of the Serra
Bicentennial Commission.*

*Bishop Thaddeus Shubsda
Episcopal Moderator*

Library of Congress Cataloging-in-Publication Data

Weber, Francis J.
    A bicentennial compendium of Maynard J. Geiger's The life
and times of Fr. Junípero Serra / by Francis J. Weber.
    106p.
    Originally published: Mission Hills, Calif. : F.J. Weber, 1984.
    ISBN 0-945-092-09-1
    1. Serra, Junipero, 1713-1784. 2.
Explorers—California—Biography. 3. Explorers—Spain—
Biography. 4. Franciscans—California—Biography.
5. California—History—To 1846.
I. Geiger, Maynard J., 1901-1977. Life and times of Fray Junípero
Serra, O.F.M. II. Title. III. Title: Life and times of Fr. Junípero
Serra. IV. Title: Life and times of Fr.ay Junípero Serra.
F864. S44W4 1988
979.4'01'0924—dc19
[B]

EZ NATURE BOOKS
P.O. Box 4206
San Luis Obispo

Preface

THIS biographical treatise is based almost exclusively on the twin volumes published in 1959 by the late Reverend Maynard J. Geiger. That outstanding Franciscan historian spent practically all his time during the eighteen years after 1941 gathering, studying then writing the life of "the man who never turned back." It was a labor of love that involved a hundred thousand miles of travel on two continents, resulting in the accumulation of over ten thousand pages of documentation.

Geiger's account is not based on multiple, yellowing pages alone, but is brightened by the author's personal knowledge of and experiences in the places where Fray Junípero Serra lived and labored. Many of its pages were written along the highways and byways, in obscure towns, in metropolitan centers, in missions and monasteries, where Serra himself had resided.

Wherever possible, Geiger tried to capture the atmosphere of Serra's day in describing the geographical setting and in reconstructing the social and religious, political and economic, as well as the institutional spirit of which Serra was a living part. In a marvelously attractive style, Geiger wedded the eighteenth to the twentieth century, thus allowing the reader to move intimately and knowingly along Serra's highroad of life through seventy full, laborious years.

Critics and reviewers alike enthusiastically welcomed the Geiger volumes. And well they might for the author was a methodical and exacting scholar in the great Germanic tradition and he rarely misfired. John Tracy Ellis once referred to Geiger's *The Life and Times of Fray Junípero Serra, O.F.M.* as the most thorough and "exasperatingly-accurate" account ever written of an American pioneer. One need only glance at the 188 pages of detailed notes in Geiger's translation of Fray Francisco Palou's *Relacion Histórica* to verify the measure of his dedication to detail.

Father Geiger often mentioned to this writer his desire that someone would come along to condense his work into a single, manageable tome, bereft of footnotes and the other encumbrances that necessarily adorned his monumental opus.

The opportunity of carrying out his wishes occurred early in 1983, when the Serra Bicentennial Commission was established by the California Catholic Conference to prepare for the 200th anniversary of Fray Junípero Serra's demise. The proposal was made then that a series of weekly newspaper essays on Serra's life be prepared for the Catholic newspapers of California. Based on Geiger's definitive work, the series ultimately grew into the present book.

The compiler wishes to thank Father Francis Guest, O.F.M., Archivist for the Santa Barbara Mission Archives and outstanding scholar in his own right, for graciously reading over this draft and offering many constructive suggestions.

It is a pleasure to publicly acknowledge the assistance of Gladys Posakony and Roberta Johnson both of whom read the galleys and offered innumerable suggestive observations.

MSGR. FRANCIS J. WEBER

Contents

Petra de Mallorca

THE Island of Mallorca in the Balearic Isles, an independent kingdom since 1229, had been united to the Spanish crown in 1479. Christianized as early as the first century after Jesus, Mallorcans customarily greeted one another with the words *"Amar a Dios!"*, a salutation subsequently made famous in faraway Alta California. In the delightful climate of Mallorca, agriculture and stock raising flourished, delectable fruits were gathered, various kinds of fish were caught, orange, almond and olive trees abounded and grape vines grew in enormous quantities.

It was into this colorful and picturesque corner of the globe, at Petra de Mallorca, that Miquel Joseph Serra was born at one o'clock on the autumn morning of November 24, 1713. (The Mallorcan *Serre* becomes *Serra* in Catalan and *Sierra* in Spanish. With a few exceptions, Junípero preferred and customarily used the Catalan spelling)

Antonio and Margarita (Ferrer) Serra lived in a small stone home at No. 5 Calle Barracar, in the southeastern and oldest section of Petra. They were of common stock of the area, industrious farmers. Neither of Serra's parents had any formal schooling. It was at home and in the fields, beside his parents, that Junípero learned something of the secrets of nature and dignity of labor.

In Mallorca, the fulfillment of the Christian duty of presenting the child for baptism was as swift as it was devout. Young Serra was brought to the parish church of Saint Peter's and there christened by Father Bartolomé Llado as Miquel Joseph Serra. (The font where Serra was baptized was removed from the church in 1858 and, for many years thereafter, was used as an ornamental flower vase in the rectory garden. In modern times, it was restored to a special chapel, with a plaque indicating its connection with Serra. It has since been located in the sanctuary.)

Visitors to Saint Peter's generally ask to see the *Registro de Bautismos* opened to Number 85 and the four line entry for Miquel

Joseph Serra. The parish priest eagerly points out the year 1713 as a special "blessing" for Mallorcans.

Returning to the Serra home, the god-parents handed the baby to his mother, with the words, "We return him to you a Christian." As soon as she was able, Margarita herself went to Saint Peter's for the "churching" of mother and child. And, if she followed another tradition of Petra, she took the first opportunity to ascend to the mountain-top shrine of Bon Any, there to dedicate the youngster to the Mother of God.

It was the practice in those times for infants to be presented for Confirmation on the occasion of the local bishop's next visitation to the parish. So it was that on May 20, 1715, Bishop Atanasio de Esterripa administered the sacrament to Miquel Joseph.

These were the humble beginnings of the man who one day would add a realm to the Church and a coastline to the Spanish empire.

Serra Joins the Franciscans

FRANCISCAN influence was strong in Petra de Mallorca during the years when Miquel Joseph Serra was growing to manhood. The youngster attended the friar's primary school at San Bernardino, where he studied religion, Latin, mathematics, reading, writing and vocal music. Because of his gifted voice, Miquel was permitted to join in chanting the Divine Office on occasion.

It was a friendly as well as formal relationship that existed between the families living on Calle Barracar and the friars. And it was this association that first sparked Miquel's interest in the Franciscan way-of-life. California obtained Serra because there was a San Bernardino.

At fifteen, Miquel decided on the service of the Church for his career. In the fall of 1729, the young man was taken to Palma, the capital, and there entrusted to one of the cathedral's canons who supervised his religious and moral training. The name of Miquel Joseph Serra was enrolled as a student of philosophy in classes conducted by the Franciscans at the Convento de San Francisco. After a year of study, he formally requested admission to the Order.

On September 14, 1730, Miquel Joseph Serra was invested with the Franciscan habit in the Convento de Santa Maria de los Angeles de Jesus. For fifty-four years, Serra would joyfully wear the garb of Francis of Assisi.

During the ensuing months, Serra underwent his basic training as a Franciscan aspirant. Prayer, meditation, choral attendance, spiritual reading, silence, promptness and physical chores were punctuated only by the festivities of an occasional feastday. Serra spent what little spare time he had delving into books of asceticism and mysticism. And he took great delight reading the chronicles of the Order which portrayed histories of the Franciscan apostolate in the Spanish provinces and homeland.

It was this reading that stirred in Serra the desire of one day being a missionary. The Spanish age of conquest in the New World was indeed a challenge to the spiritually venturesome. And while his initial burst of enthusiasm for an active missionary life was submerged by obedience, it never died.

Serra himself chose the religious name of "Junípero." (The original Junípero was a companion to Francis of Assisi—the "Jester of God," a man of utter simplicity and celestial mirth.) When his novitiate was nearing completion, Serra cheerfully made the decision to bind himself irrevocably to God and the service of the Franciscan Order. And so, at the age of eighteen, on September 15, 1731, Miquel became Fray Junípero Serra.

From then on Serra was a Franciscan forever, known in ecclesial annals as Junípero. Each year, on April 16th, Serra renewed his vows, recapturing the jubilant feeling of that inspiring ceremony at the Convento de Jesus. Shortly afterwards, Serra moved to the Convento de San Francisco, close to the sea and the cathedral. There he had another six years of studying philosophy and theology in preparation for ordination to the priesthood.

The Professorial Years

D URING the eighteen years that Fray Junípero Serra lived, worked and prayed at the Convento de San Francisco, Palma de Mallorca, books and study dominated the major portion of his time. Late in 1731, Serra received tonsure and the minor orders, the first steps to ordination. Then came the copious classes in theology required for reception of the ministerial priesthood.

Serra was ordained deacon on Saint Patrick's Day, 1736, but the exact date of his advancement to priesthood is unrecorded. His biographer suggests that the event took place just prior to Christmas, 1737, when Serra had reached the prescribed canonical age.

Aware of his pedagogical talents, Serra's superiors singled him out to be a professor within the Seraphic Order. After passing the necessary examinations, Fray Junípero Serra was awarded the coveted title "lector of philosophy." Serra began his professorial career early in 1740. Fortunately, one of his students kept a careful written transcript of Serra's lectures which is still extant. It numbered no fewer than 808 pages!

According to the transcription, Serra concluded the three year course with personal note of deep spiritual import:

> I desire nothing more of you than this that when the news of my death shall have reached your ears, I ask that you say for the benefit of my soul "May he rest in peace," and I shall not fail to do the same for you so that all of us will attain that goal for which we have been created. Amen and farewell. . . . I am no longer your professor but your most humble servant.

In 1743, a year after receiving his doctorate, Serra was named to the Chair of Scotistic Theology at the Lullian University.

During his tenure in that prestigious assignment, Fray Junípero Serra took preaching appointments in various parts of Mallorca.

Serra was as accomplished at preaching as he was at teaching. Sprung from the country soil himself, he never lost the ability to touch his simple hearers. Generally, he preached in the Mallorcan dialect, which was akin to Catalan. His easy eloquence, resonant voice and fiery earnestness won Serra many listeners in academic circles too. His biographer recalled one panegyric delivered on January 25, 1749:

> Everyone was full of admiration. With my own ears I heard one of his listeners, a professor and brilliant preacher who was himself a little jealous . . . exclaiming, "There is a sermon that deserves to be printed in letters of gold."

In June of 1743, Serra was singularly honored by being invited to preach on the Feast of *Corpus Christi* in Palma's historic cathedral. That event was traditionally among the more memorable of local celebrations and only the most outstanding speakers were asked to participate. By all the reasonable standards, Fray Junípero Serra, now in his early thirties, had achieved all any friar could ever have anticipated. And there was promise of future advancement in the ranks of his own Order. Seemingly none of that interested him.

In the midst of this well-ordered and useful existence, Fray Junípero Serra reviewed his life and thought about the years ahead. He could not have known then that the Californias figured into his future.

Departure
for the New World

L ATE in 1748, after much prayer and deliberation, Fray Junípero Serra wrote to the Commissary General of the Indies, asking permission for himself and Fray Francisco Palóu to become apostolic missionaries. On Palm Sunday, a special messenger arrived at the Convento de San Francisco with official authorization for the two friars to join a group of missionaries bound for the West Indies.

Two weeks later, the friars bade farewell to their confreres, and made their way to Palma's harbor, where they boarded an English ship for the first leg of their lengthy journey. On May 2nd, they left Malaga and cruised along the hill-fringed coast of southern Spain, passing the formidable rock of Gibraltar. Five days later, they rounded the peninsula on which Cadiz is located and entered the historic harbor.

There, the friars met the others who had responded from all parts of Spain to the call for evangelizing the New World. It was while waiting at Cadiz that Fray Junípero Serra wrote a letter to the parish priest at Petra, asking that he inform his parents about his becoming a missionary.

That letter, referred to by one writer as the *"magna carta* of Serra's apostolate,"* reveals the friar at life's crossroads, a man who in strength of character, assisted by grace, made the irrevocable decision to leave aging parents, beloved homeland, associations of youth, cloister and community, books and university, honor and future renown for a spiritual motive based on the Gospel. By absorbing the message of that letter, one can understand the Junípero of the future.

Serra asked the priest to tell his parents about the "great joy" that filled his heart at becoming a missionary. Knowing that, "surely they would always encourage me to go forward and never to turn back. Let them remember that the office of an apostolic preacher, especially in its actual exercise, is the greatest calling to which they could wish me to be chosen.

"Since they are advanced in years, let them recall that life is uncertain and, in fact, may be very brief. . . . Since this is true, it will be very much to the point and most conformable to the holy will of God if they will not emphasize the very little help that I could give them with regard to the needs of this life. Rather they should strive to merit from God, our Lord, that if we see each other no more in this life, we may be joined forever in future glory.

"Let them rejoice that they have a son who is a priest, though an unworthy one and a sinner, who daily in the holy sacrifice of the Mass prays for them with all the fervor of his soul and on many days applies the Mass for them alone, so that the Lord may aid them. . . . If I, by the grace of God, succeed in becoming a good religious, my prayers will become more efficacious, and they in consequence will be the gainers.

"The same I say to my beloved sister in Christ, Juana, and to my brother-in-law, Miquel. Let them not be concerned about me now, but rather let them commend me to God that I may be a good priest and a holy minister of God.

"In this we are all very interested and this alone matters. I recall the occasion when my father was so ill that extreme unction was administered to him. I, being a religious, was at home at the time, and thinking that he was going to die, we two being alone, he said to me: 'My son, let me charge you to be a good religious of your Father, St. Francis.'

"Now, dear father, be assured that those words are as fresh in my memory as when they proceeded from your lips. Realize, too, that in order to become a good religious, I have set out on this course."

Across the Sea

THE ship *Villasota,* also known as *Nuestra Señora de Guadalupe,* departed from Cadiz at the end of August, 1749. Aboard was Fray Junípero Serra and nineteen other Franciscans bound for the missions.

After a fairly peaceful journey at sea, the ship arrived at San Juan, Puerto Rico, on the feast of Saint Luke. Serra's first hours in the New World were spent at the hermitage of the Immaculate Conception, near the walls of the city.

Puerto Rico was not to be a vacation land for the friars. He and the others were full of zeal and their first hours on American soil demonstrated their selfless industry. The friars utilized their time by conducting a mission for the islanders. It proved to be the first outlet for Serra's apostolic work in America. The cathedral was jammed to capacity. It had been nine years since a similar religious service had been held in San Juan and the local populace anxiously responded to the opportunity of renewing their spiritual lives.

The *Villasota* left San Juan on November 1st. For another month the ship sailed through the islands and reefs of the Caribbean. There were many hardships during that sojurn, the worst of which was the critical shortage of drinking water. Serra is recorded as having noted to a companion that "the best way of saving one's saliva is to eat little and talk still less."

His biographer notes that during the long voyage Serra "was always even tempered and smiling, that he never uttered the slightest complaint, that his patience was the wonder and admiration of everyone." Anchor was cast in the historic harbor of Vera Cruz, where Mexican history began, on December 6th.

On the following day, Serra stepped on the continental soil of North America for the first time at "the most desired end of a long and tedious voyage." From that American counterpart of the Spanish Cadiz, Serra and his companions would spread across the great viceroyalty of New Spain.

A thanksgiving celebration took place and Fray Junípero was chosen to preach at the Solemn High Mass. With his good memory for detail, he recalled the full details of their ninety-nine day voyage and the petitions to Santa Barbara for a successful arrival. During his short homily, Serra spiritualized the entire voyage with the protecting mantle of God's providence. Again his native talent and eloquence were revealed, although time and oblivion deny us the privilege of catching something of his feeling and fire. Today, the little chapel of *Santo Cristo del Buen Viaje* (the Holy Christ of the Safe Voyage) remains as a reminder of the days when travel was perilous and uncertain and prayer was a part of everyone's itinerary.

At Vera Cruz, men of war and men of peace, soldiers of the king and soldiers of the cross, started out on their missions of force or persuasion. There began *El Camino Real* of the New World. There Fray Junípero Serra started out on the trail that would culminate in Alta California.

Mexico City

THE *Camino Real* which connected Vera Cruz with Mexico City stretched from sea level to an altitude of 7,382 feet, through tropical country, arid plains, high plateaus, across formidable *sierras*, in view of volcanoes and lakes, perennial snow and abundant sunshine.

Though horses were available for the journey, Fray Junípero Serra and a companion from Andalusia decided to walk to Mexico City. In so doing, Serra identified with the *friales andariegos* (the walking friars) who were famous in the New World. The two friars began their journey without money or guide. Their breviaries were their sole possessions. They knew they could rely on the native Indian and Spanish hospitality which was still the unwritten law of the land.

Walking between fifteen and twenty miles each day, the missionaries set out after Mass. They took a *siesta* at midday when the sun was warm and the travel most weary. Their lodging and food was sought *por amor de Dios* (for the love of God). New geography lessons and whole chapters of nomenclature and practical Christian charity were to be learned all along the way.

During the trek, Serra's leg became swollen and he was plagued with a burning itch. He attributed the swelling to a mosquito bite, though it may have been inflicted by a chigger common to that area and other tropical regions. It was a wound that would plague him the rest of his life, at times causing critical pain.

Though he left no record of his first impressions of America as he trudged along *El Camino Real*, Serra certainly saw and experienced much that was new and different from Mallorca. He passed lush vegetation and semi-arid plants; incipient as well as spent volcanoes; fierce-looking lava deposits; marshes and formidable river torrents; magnificent, towering mountains; strange-looking people in *ponchos* and *guaraches*; primitive, lonely shacks and terrible roads. And, socially, he was in another world. Though it had the unmistakable Spanish impress upon it, it was primarily Indian territory. It was New Spain where nature took on magnitude.

With new vision and high hopes, Fray Junípero Serra came hobbling painfully into Mexico City, his new home. He arrived at the shrine of Our Lady of Guadalupe, the religious hearth of Mexico, on the evening of December 31st and there he remained overnight with prayers of gratitude to the Blessed Mother.

Serra arrived at San Fernando College on New Year's day. He had traveled from Bon Any in Mallorca to the hill of Tepeyac in Mexico, the chain of his travels linked two sacred hills dedicated to the Madonna he loved and revered. He was now six thousand miles from home. San Fernando was one of the leading apostolic colleges in the New World whose purpose was the formation of able missionaries. It was an independent, specialized institution within the framework of the Franciscan Order where friars were trained for the apostolate of the home missions and the unconverted Indian field.

Here, in a sense, it was journey's end for Serra. In another sense, his road of life was just beginning.

Sierra Gorda Missions

A FTER some months of intensive missionary preparation at San Fernando, Serra and a number of other friars were appointed to the Sierra Gorda region of Mexico, located in the heart of the Sierra Madre Oriental. In that vast mountainous area lived the half-wild Pames Indians. The valleys there are few and small and the arable land is studded with rocks. Then and now life in the Sierra Gorda is rugged and unpredictable, day or night, the year around.

At the time of Serra's arrival, Christianity had touched the Pamas but little. Those few who had been baptized were poorly instructed. The economic and spiritual conditions that Fray Junípero Serra found in Jalpan were anything but promising. Serra found about one thousand "practicing" Catholics in the region. With Fray Francisco Palóu, his assistant, he set out to learn the language of the Pames—a challenge that taxed the Mallorcan's intellectual talents.

When he was sufficiently proficient, Serra translated the body of Christian doctrine and a number of traditional prayers into Pame. Before long, he was able to preach in the language and this together with his gentle example won them over to a more civilized and Christian form of life.

Serra had a sense of the dramatic and he used it to good advantage. Occasionally, for example, he would go to confession in the sanctuary of the Church in full view of the congregation, an action that had a telling effect on even the simplest mind. By example, persuasion and eloquent preaching, Fray Junípero succeeded in bringing the Indians around to their Catholic obligations so that nearly all complied with the minimum duty of the Paschal precept.

Serra motivated the Indians to worship God by providing for them the splendor of the liturgy. The major feasts were solemnized with ceremonies and devotions. Christmas was celebrated in the

Franciscan fashion by a mystery play similar to those of his native Petra, enacted by the children whom he trained for the purpose. And so on throughout the whole liturgical season.

With this untutored people of the hills, Serra realized that visual expression of religion in dramatic form was of prime importance. If such expression was of significance in Mallorca after nearly a thousand years of Christianity, it was still more important in the *sierra* where the faith was only taking root.

Fray Junípero began his ministry in the Sierra Gorda as missionary pastor of Jalpan. In 1751, he was named *presidente* of the Sierra Gorda missions, a position he held for three years. During his tenure, Serra visited the missions of his area, to comfort and sustain the friars, to oversee the general progress and to chide or encourage as the case warranted. Several times during that time he was required to visit Mexico City on business.

Ever so gradually, the friar put into operation the rules drawn up by Fray Pedro Perez de Mezquia and those regulations were to become the blueprint for all the missions sponsored by the colleges of Querétaro, San Fernando and Zacatecas. Their influence was to reach as far as San Francisco in Alta California.

Priest Among the People

A T Jalpan, Father Serra worked for economic betterment, realizing that the more progressive it was, the more stable and beneficent would be his religious ministrations. The harvests each year under his administration were not only sufficient, but sometimes abundant.

The Indians were given their own parcels of land to produce corn, beans and pumpkins; occasionally they were presented with a yoke of oxen and seeds for planting. Women were taught spinning, knitting and sewing. The Indians were encouraged to sell their wares at places like Zimapan, a mining center.

Before leaving the Sierra Gorda, Serra proposed the notion of constructing a large stone church, ample enough to hold the entire congregation. Work on the edifice was scheduled for those periods of the year when the Indians were not attending to their fields.

The friar worked alongside the laborers. In his torn gray habit, no one would have recognized the ex-professor of theology at the Lullian University among the crew of workers. It took seven years to complete the church which is still used for divine worship by the descendants of the 18th century Pames. The church at Jalpan is the one remaining piece of Serra's building program during his missionary career—the mission buildings of California built under his years of presidency, with the exception of the adobe chapel at Capistrano, having given way to worthier structures.

During those same years, the missionaries working under Serra's supervision erected stone churches at four other locations. Those monuments remain on the hillsides to attest to the work of Junípero Serra in establishing the faith in the Sierra Gorda.

In 1758, Serra was recalled to Mexico City for re-assignment. He surely left the area with some degree of accomplishment, knowing that economic conditions had been bettered, religion was on a higher plane, splendid churches had been built, the majority of the Indians had become practical Catholics and were absorbing the essentials of a stable civilized life based on the Spanish pattern.

Today the descendants of the Pimas are faithful worshippers in the churches built by their forefathers. The faith of the *sierra*, as well as the churches, is a monument to the zeal of Serra and his confreres.

For a while it looked as if Serra would be sent to the Texas missions where only recently the Indians had unleashed a general massacre, killing one friar and injuring several others. The death of the viceroy, however, changed those plans.

From 1758 to 1767, Fray Junípero Serra was bound up in the internal life of San Fernando, serving the college in various capacities unrelated to Indian missions. It has been estimated that he travelled by foot no less than 5,500 miles giving missions during those years—considerable exercise for a man with foot and leg ulcers!

Serra's life at San Fernando was made more austere by personal choice rather than by the rules of the Institute. Even as a youth, Serra had been serious, a quality he retained all through his life. Austerities added to a natural seriousness made him appear aloof and somewhat unapproachable. Yet he had a kindliness of spirit that became apparent as soon as one talked with him. His many penances and prayers did not destroy in him a sense of humor, and the human pleasantry he possessed is apparent in his many letters.

Call to California

ON February 27, 1767, King Charles III abruptly expelled the Society of Jesus from Spain and its colonies. The king's action was distinctly unpopular, but viceroys, governors, soldiers and missionaries had learned to be silent and obedient to their monarch.

Shortly after the announcement that the Society was to leave the uninviting Peninsula of Baja California, a decision was made to entrust the orphaned Jesuit missions there to the Franciscans of the Apostolic College of San Fernando. Though college officials had little enthusiasm for the undertaking, they had no choice in the matter. Fray Junípero Serra was among the friars chosen for the new apostolate and he was also to serve as *Presidente* of the missions.

In mid July, the small missionary contingency bade farewell to their community. Just before leaving, the superior briefly addressed the group: "Go forth with the blessing of God and Our Seraphic Father, Saint Francis, to evangelize that mystic field of labor in California entrusted to us by our Catholic Sovereign. Go forth with the comforting thought that you have as your superior, Father Lector Junípero, whom by these letters patent I name president of all Your Reverences and of the missions."

On April 2nd, the friars disembarked at Loreto, the unpretentious capital of Baja California. The humble church in which they were to begin their work as successors of the Jesuits was a plain, flat-roofed building with a ceiling formed of nicely worked beams of cedar wood.

Governor Gaspar de Portolá welcomed the friars. On April 3rd, they celebrated Easter with all becoming solemnity. Fifteen priests said their Masses early in the morning and later Fray Junípero Serra offered the Solemn Mass, with the others forming the choir. After Mass, the *Alabado* was sung.

Having learned the location, distance and needs of each mission, Serra proceeded to assign his subjects to them. Though all were pleased, none knew exactly what his mission in this rough country among the poverty-stricken Indians would be like. Serra outlined a uniform method of administering the missions and then gave his subjects a paternal talk about their future work, urging all of them to labor zealously in their new vineyards.

The Indian population at some of the missions was very small; in all of them there were only 7, 149 Indians of all ages. Some had sufficient water from small streams, but droughts were common and the periodic locust plagues were devastating. When the harvest was good, the products included wheat, corn, beans, rice, figs, olives, pomegranates, peaches, watermelons, pumpkins, lemons, oranges, bananas and cotton.

The early months were times of appraisal, adjustment and rudimentary labor, each missionary having to shift for himself. It was incumbent upon them to learn the local dialects, even though Spanish was spoken in sections.

To a great extent, the peninsula of Baja California is a forbidding stretch of land projecting itself in a southwesterly direction deep in the Pacific. Even today, it has little to offer except to those tied to it by circumstance of birth or to outsiders filled with the spirit of adventure.

Glance at the Vineyard

IN the mid 18th century, Baja California was described as a land fit for three types of people: missionaries who, for the love of God and charity toward their neighbor, left the cultural ties of their homeland and elected to live in isolation and discomfort on a cheerless frontier to accomplish some spiritual good; Spaniards born in America who could make a living nowhere else and were useful there as cowboys and muleteers; the native Indians who knew no better and apparently were perfectly satisfied to be left alone.

The Jesuits had built some sort of a road connecting most of the missions but even they would not have boasted of its quality. It barely served the riders and the zealous missionaries of the time.

The natives of Baja California were at a primitive cultural level, for they lived solely by hunting, fishing and seed gathering and had neither letters, agriculture nor architecture. Anthropologists called such people lower nomads or marginal peoples. They were forced by circumstances to roam about within restricted areas to obtain their food.

Their menu included such things as roots, grasses and seeds, birds, horses, burros, mules, dogs, cats, rats, mice, snakes and bats; walnut leaves and certain types of edible wood; leather cured and uncured; the bones of birds, sheep, goats and calves. Fish and meat already putrid were eaten without discrimination.

The men went about completely naked, while the women wore clothing made of fibers and skins. Girls were taught how to make these coverings and children were expected to shift for themselves as soon as possible.

No basic education was given to the children; for the most part they were allowed to do as they pleased. The boys learned how to make the bow and arrow, for the Indians, even in the mission period, always carried these arms, more valuable to them than a knife and fork in so sterile a country. The shortage of water was a problem; urine was used to wash the face where water was lacking.

The Indians were well-proportioned people, of good presence, agile and fearless. Some were quick to learn, others hopelessly slow at acquiring new skills. They were great conversationalists with a sense of humor and a fund of jokes. A variety of dialects was found among them. The languages lacked expressions for Christian ideas and abstract concepts. It took no little ingenuity on the part of the missionaries to compose even the Lord's Prayer in the local dialects.

There was always an economic problem at the missions, despite the great efforts of the Jesuits to impart and apply European agricultural method to the stubborn New World soil. There was never enough food to go around; so the Indians were permitted to hunt on their own to supplement the mission produce. The lack of food made it impossible to gather all the Indians into the mission settlements and this factor retarded their effective culturalization.

Though Christianity had been propagated for over sixty years in the peninsula, there was still much to be done. Most of the Indians south of Santa Maria de los Angeles had come under Christian influences.

To this land and to these people came Fray Junípero Serra and his companions. When José de Galvez arrived, soon thereafter, he expected to find a miniature paradise on the peninsula. In his attempts to make over the area, he simply complicated the burdens of the missionaries.

Operation Alta California

JOSÉ de Galvez was sent to Mexico by King Charles III for the purpose of making an official visitation of the entire viceroyalty. He arrived in 1765 and remained until 1771, years in which he gained a wide knowledge of the extensive area. Interested in knowing all about the details of missionary operations, Galvez wrote to the friars, asking for reports of their charges. With that information before him, he would then make an investigation of conditions himself.

Fray Junípero Serra made out his report and forwarded it to Galvez. Then the friar started out on a tour of three missions to the north, probably to get a better idea of them himself and also to talk over future expansion of the apostolate. Galvez was unhappy about certain aspects of the temporal operations then being followed. Even before all the reports had come in, he had determined to turn the mission temporalities over to the Franciscans. He felt this measure necessary to save the foundations economically.

On August 12, 1768, Galvez signed a decree authorizing the missionaries to assume complete control of their establishments. He thus entrusted Serra and his co-workers with the difficult task of bringing order out of chaos and prosperity from ruination.

Throughout his years on the peninsula, Galvez kept in close touch with Serra. His appreciation of the Franciscan apostolate is obvious in a letter to the viceroy, wherein he says that "in the charity and zeal of the apostolic ministers who are in charge of the missions of this peninsula, I have found all the cooperation necessary to satisfy my desires."

When José de Galvez told Serra of his determination to occupy Alta California, the Mallorcan friar immediately offered to go in person as the first volunteer "to erect the holy standard of the cross in Monterey." He assured Galvez that other missionaries would not be lacking to join in that great enterprise.

This was the opportunity Serra had longed and prayed for—to reach pagan land and plant there the Faith on unworked soil. It was, after all, the reason Serra had come to America.

Galvez and Serra planned carefully for the expedition that would thrust European presence into Alta California. It was decided, for example, that the existing peninsular missions would contribute sufficient material from church and sacristy for the first three foundations.

On January 9, 1769, the *San Carlos* was ready to set out from La Paz. Galvez, Serra and the others were on hand. Galvez told the group that it was being sent out in the name of God, the king and the viceroy to plant the standard of the Holy Cross among the heathen of New California. He charged them to preserve peace among themselves and to respect and revere their chaplain. Serra blessed the ship, its chaplain, crew and twenty-five soldiers under the command of Lieutenant Pedro Fages. The *San Carlos* weighed anchor on schedule and sailed to Cape San Lucas, there to start its voyage along the Pacific.

A month later, similar departure ceremonies were observed for the *San Antonio*. Operation Alta California was in motion.

Rim of Christendom

THE third expeditionary force, the first to travel overland, departed for Alta California in mid-March of 1769. Fray Junípero Serra was to accompany the fourth and final arm of the expedition which was scheduled to leave from Loreto. Gaspar de Portolá was commander and Serra chaplain and diarist.

In the opening words of his account, Serra set the tone by observing that it was a journey undertaken "for the greater glory of God and the conversion of the pagans to our holy Catholic faith." To Serra, the faith was a gift and he was determined to share it with others. When hesitation was expressed about Serra's ability to withstand the rigors of travel, because of his infected foot and leg, the decision was made to also assign Fray Miguel de la Campa to accompany the expedition. Serra would join them on the frontier.

Meanwhile, officials at San Fernando College had named Fray Francisco Palóu as *presidente* for Baja California, an appointment that would become effective the moment Serra left the frontier for the north. Serra had been careful to provide for the spiritualities of the peninsular missions after his departure.

When at last he was able to travel, it was necessary that two men lift Serra onto his mule and adjust him in the saddle. Few would have imagined that the determined friar was destined to work yet another fifteen years, accomplishing much for the Lord along *El Camino Real*. The worn-out mule and aging *padre* made their painful way from Loreto to the north. Throughout the journey, Serra kept a meticulous diary, the most valuable and surely the longest document he ever wrote.

At San Borja Mission, Serra was enthusiastically welcomed by Fray Fermín Francisco de Lasuén who would oneday succeed him as *presidente* of the Alta California missions. The two friars spent several days planning for the present and anticipating the future. On May day, Serra moved on toward the frontier mission of

Santa Maria and there, on the rim of Christendom, he caught up with Gaspar de Portolá, de la Campa and other members of the expedition.

On May 13th, the small contingency arrived at Velicatá where, on the Feast of Pentecost, Serra founded his first mission. A cross was raised, bells were rung and Holy Mass was offered under the patronage of San Fernando. Few missions have been founded in such impoverished circumstances. As Serra himself noted, the celebration took place "with all the neatness of holy poverty." Several days later, when a number of Indians appeared on the scene, Serra explained the reason for his presence among them.

Early in June, the Gaspar de Portolá expedition reached San Diego, where they were heartened at seeing the *San Carlos* and the *San Antonio* riding at anchor near the mouth of the bay. Serra recorded in his diary that "it was a day of great rejoicing and merriment for all. . . . And although this sort of consolation appears to be the solace of the miserable, for us it was the source of happiness."

Serra was especially jubilant. He had traveled nine hundred miles from Loreto, two thousand miles from San Fernando, eight thousand miles from Mallorca, to reach Alta California. Now he was in the beautiful harbor of San Diego on the Pacific, ready to raise aloft the cross of Christ.

Saint Joseph
to the Rescue

NO one can stand on Presidio Hill in San Diego and remain unmoved by the fact that here is the cradle of Christianity and civilization in California. In 1769, the area was still untrodden by Christian feet.

Within a radius of ten leagues of San Diego, there were about twenty Indian villages. Frequent battles had taken place among them. Each village was governed by a chief who had but one wife at a time but dismissed her at will. Marriage followed after the groom requested the bride from the parents. At death the body was cremated amongst much weeping and the throwing of seed.

The wizards or medicine men pretended to cure their patients by sucking the affected parts and extracting objects from their own mouths as if they came from the wound or sore. Upon this primitive culture the missionaries had to erect a civilized community.

The immediate outlook at San Diego was bleak. The area's first institution was not a mission or *presidio*, but an infirmary. Twenty-one sailors and several soldiers died from scurvy and most of the survivors were ill and unfit for work. Provisions were short and several Indians on the Rivera expedition had died from hunger. The lifeline of the Spanish empire along the Californias was certainly a slender thread.

In his first letter from Alta California, Fray Junípero Serra had a timely piece of advice and warning.

Let those who are to come here as missionaries not imagine that they are coming for any other purpose but to endure hardships for the love of God and for the salvation of souls.

Serra turned his attention to the establishment of the mission atop Presidio Hill. On the morning of July 16th, feast of Our Lady of Mount Carmel, the soldiers raised the cross and Serra blessed it.

Christianity was officially implanted in California by a few intrepid men.

The first months were unrewarding. Serra described them as a period during which he could do no more than prepare the groundwork of the elements for conversion. The local Indians frequently visited the mission and the *padres* gave them trinkets and gifts to win their good will. As the months progressed, great concern was felt at San Diego over the shortage of supplies. Portolá told Serra that if the *San Antonio* did not arrive by March 19th, the foundation would have to be abandoned.

The idea of leaving San Diego was a blow to Serra. He feared that if they departed, San Diego might never again be occupied and the conversion of the Indians would never take place. He had staked his life and health on the venture. His whole nature rebelled against giving up. His natural tenacity combined with his faith in God urged him to find a way to remain.

Early in March, Serra proposed that a novena of prayers be inaugurated to insure the arrival of the *San Antonio*. The nine days that followed were perhaps the most anxious of the friar's life. About three o'clock in the afternoon of Saint Joseph's day, the almost unbelievable happened—on the horizon beyond the Silver Gate, the sails of a ship were described.

The sight of that sail prevented the march south and the abandonment of San Diego, for supplies had come to California. Serra's determination and his confidence in God's timely aid had won the right to stay and plant the cross.

On to Monterey

NOW that San Diego had been reinforced by the arrival of the *San Antonio*, soldiers and missionaries began planning for further expansion. The initial step would be a sea and land trek to Monterey. Serra opted for the former. After a long and "somewhat uncomfortable voyage", Serra and the crew members of the *San Antonio* arrived at Monterey on June 1st, there to rendezvous with the overland party which had completed their journey several days earlier.

It was readily agreed that the formal establishment of San Carlos Borromeo Mission would take place on Pentecost Sunday, June 3rd. Early that day, Gaspar de Portolá and the others gathered under a mighty oak by a ravine running into the bay.

It was thought that this tree was the same one under which the Carmelites with Sebastian Vizcaíno in 1602 said the first Mass in the area. Again it was chosen as the site for the Eucharistic Liturgy. Serra relates that after Mass Portolá observed a nicety of protocol by declaring that the "primary purpose" of the king was to extend the faith, so the cross should precede the flag. For that reason, Serra first erected the cross and founded the mission; then there followed the act of taking possession.

There was also a somber note of mourning in the day's otherwise joyous festivities. One of the sailors had died aboard ship the preceding day. Serra assisted at the funeral services and the remains were buried at the foot of the mission cross.

Next day, the site for the *presidio*-mission was chosen: a flat piece of land near the ocean, some distance east of the ravine and the oak. Serra called it "a pleasing stretch of land." Easily identifiable today, it is near the present site of the old *presidio* church still standing in the city of Monterey.

From the very outset, Fray Junípero Serra realized that while San Carlos Mission began at Monterey, the permanent site could not be there. The first ingredient for a mission was lacking: the presence of a large Indian town, as required by the laws of the Indies. There was timber there, but no good drinking water.

On June 14th, the Feast of *Corpus Christi* was observed. The celebration was a relief from the makeshift life they had all been leading. Serra may have magnified its beauty but to him it was real. He wrote that "it was carried out indeed with such splendor that it could have been witnessed with pleasure had it taken place in Mexico."

In a letter written to officials at the Apostolic College of San Fernando, Serra repeated his qualifications for future priestly volunteers in the area: "Those who come here dedicated to so holy a work must undergo sacrifices, as everyone knows. . . . In these distant parts, one must expect to suffer some hardships, but these will be even more burdensome to those who are seeking every convenience and comfort." Serra obviously wanted men who were every inch apostles and he looked forward to the day when more missionaries would come and all would enjoy the "worthwhile benefits of mutual encouragement, security and solidarity."

What Fray Junípero Serra looked for in others was, in himself, taken for granted.

Word Reaches Homefront

IN a little over a year, the Spanish realm along the shores of the Pacific had been extended over eight hundred miles, from San Fernando de Velicatá to Monterey, and three missions and two *presidios* had been established in the area. When news of the event reached Mexico City, everyone was jubilant. The church of the city rang their bells and the massed clangor sounded like Rome after a canonization. San Fernando, with greater claim than all the others, joined in the common jubilee, for two of her sons, Frays Junípero Serra and Juan Crespi, had planted the cross over two thousand miles away.

The excited populace soon learned the significance of it all. A Solemn Mass of thanksgiving was offered in the Metropolitan Cathedral, with both the Visitor General and Viceroy in attendance. In his official statement, the Viceroy did not overlook Fray Junípero Serra's part in the dramatic occurrence, noting that the "exemplary and zealous missionary" had related the events surrounding the Christian penetration of Alta California.

On October 25, 1770, thirty additional missionaries (twenty for Baja and ten for Alta California) left the Apostolic College of San Fernando. The new guardian at the college was Fray Rafael Verger and it was he who would act as Serra's superior in those formative years. Verger appreciated that he had an excellent field commander in Alta California. Concerning Serra, he wrote that the *Presidente* "was held in high esteem because of his learning and remarkable talents," he had come to the New World to "teach the benighted pagans of this vast kingdom the catechism and Christian doctrine."

Verger and Serra were a naturally compatible unit. The two sons of Mallorcan farmers were plowing for God and Spain but both often found the ground stubborn and unreceptive.

It must be understood that the spiritual and temporal conquest of California was controlled by an interlocking directorate of

Church and state. The king, the Council of the Indies, the Board of Trade, the viceroy, military governor, local *presidio* commander, the Commissary General of the Indies, the guardian at the Apostolic College of San Fernando all jostled with the *Presidente* in furthering the interests of both Church and state.

The union was intimate in theory and practice. The organization was tightly knit on the highest level in Spain, on the intermediate level in Mexico and on the lower level in California. Little deviation from set rules was allowed and little individual enterprise was permitted.

All these officials worked hand-in-hand, sometimes harmoniously, sometimes at variance. Misunderstandings arose from variant interpretations of the law without the contestants being able to consult higher authority readily. Disputes came when clashing personalities insisted on their rights, feigned or real.

The poor communications of the age and the tremendous distances involved stagger our imagination today. It took nearly a year, for example, to ask a question and receive an answer. The whole scheme worked out simply because hardy and zealous men in uniform and habit, real frontiersmen and pioneers, serving God and the king, striving to be good Christians and remaining very human in many things, bearing arms and shouldering the Cross, were willing to undergo privations and hardships to attain their goal.

Time Marches On

L IKE most great leaders, Fray Junípero Serra was impatient. He once observed that "I do not say that everything must be done in one day but I do think that the ship should sail when the wind is favorable."

Progress at Monterey must have been excruciatingly slow by Serra's standards. It was only on December 26, 1770 that the *Presidente* performed his first baptism there. By the following May, twenty Indians had been received into the Church, but it was a long process catechizing them.

The arrival of ten additional friars in March of the following year augured well for it meant that the founding of new missions would not be long delayed. On July 8th, for example, Serra, two of his fellow friars, seven soldiers, three sailors and a few Indians from peninsular California left Monterey for the Valley of the Bears in the Sierra de Santa Lucia. Studded with oaks, the valley had a river running through it that was filled with water even during July. Serra chose a spot upon which the Mission of San Antonio de Padua should be temporarily founded—leaving the exact locale of the mission's future site to circumstances.

The bells were hung from an oak and an improvised altar was set up in an *enramada* on the Feast of Saint Bonaventure. In the beautiful sun-warmed valley of the oaks, Serra was seized with rapturous enthusiasm. He began to ring the bells and to them added the evangel of his clarion voice: "Come, you pagans; come to the Holy Church; come, come to receive the Faith of Jesus Christ!"

For the next eight days the soldiers worked at building the necessary shelters for themselves and the missionaries and on the following Sunday Mass was offered for the first time in the improvised chapel which Serra had determined upon as the correct site for the mission.

The account of Serra's enthusiasm at the establishment of the mission is in accord with his fervid character and his missionary zeal. Given the valley's picturesque setting and the long-enforced idleness at Monterey, no doubt he gave full vent to his pent-up emotions. Returning to Monterey, Serra set about transferring San Carlos Borromeo from the *presidio* to the banks of the Carmel River, with its view of the beautiful bay and rocky Point Lobos. On August 24th, he blessed the cross and sang the first Mass on the site.

Frays Pedro Benito Cambon and Angel Somera were appointed by Serra to establish the mission named for San Gabriel where the Montebello hills enclose the southern boundary of the San Miguel Valley. That site too was well chosen. There was plentiful water for irrigation and nearby, to the east, were the San Gabriel and Rio Hondo rivers. There was a dense oak forest to the northwest which supplied abundant acorns for the Indians and wood for the mission.

The initial buildings at San Gabriel were completed in the shortest possible time. Unhappily, it was not long before dark shadows fell over San Gabriel. An altercation between the soldiers and the Indians occurred during which the local chief was killed. That unfortunate event, coupled with the immoral conduct of several soldiers, caused great anxiety for Serra and the other missionaries. How any conversions at San Gabriel were effected under such circumstances is little short of miraculous.

Gradually, with the transferral of the more unsavory soldiers, the moral climate improved and, as Serra reported to the Viceroy, "the *padres* began to breathe easier after their long period of affliction."

Return to Capital

ON August 24, 1772, the first anniversary of the planting of the Cross in the Carmel Valley, Fray Junípero Serra, Pedro Fages and several others left Monterey for San Diego. It was to be Serra's first overland trip along California's *El Camino Real.* On this trip he came to know the complete coast of California from Monterey south and made mental notes that helped him fashion his chain or ladder of missions. Much of what Serra saw on the trip determined his future course of action.

At San Antonio, Serra found a small Christian community of about a dozen Indians. The *Presidente* was encouraged and realized that as soon as the food situation became better and the undesirable soldiers were removed, San Antonio would become a model outpost. The party moved on south and on September 1st, on the slope of a hill within the shadow of San Luis Obispo Peak, Serra raised the cross of California's fifth mission. Fray Jose Cavaller was left behind as resident missionary.

Circumstances dictated leaving only a handful of guards at San Luis Obispo and Serra noted later that it would have been a foolhardy venture had it been for any reason other than the sheer love to convert the Indians. Fortunately, as he said, God "did not abandon the agents of so holy an enterprise."

On September 11th, the party arrived at San Gabriel, and Serra was able to personally see the mission for the first time. He was delighted with the place and the progress that had been made. Though he remained only two days, Serra declared that it was "without doubt the most excellent mission site so far discovered. Once it is sufficiently developed, it will be able, doubtless, to sustain not only itself, but all the rest." By the time of his arrival at San Diego, the *Presidente* had seen nearly five hundred miles of new territory. He now had a better perspective and a fuller knowledge of his extensive mission field.

Ever so gradually, the relationship between Governor Pedro Fages and Fray Junípero Serra began deteriorating. Lines of authority were not well drawn and even more poorly interpreted. Serra found himself at the crossroads of the mission enterprise. The vexations, delays, bickerings, misunderstandings and restrictions of the past two years had come to a peak in San Diego. The major question then was—would he go ahead, stand still or retreat?

On October 13th, the *Presidente* met with the missionaries at San Diego and stated his opinion that one of them should go to Mexico in person to see the Viceroy and lay the whole matter of mission administration before him. The friars agreed and decided that Serra was the person to go unless his age and infirmities prevented him from doing so.

Inasmuch as the *San Carlos* was then in the harbor, the *Presidente* decided to leave on the ship when it left for San Blas. As his companion for the long journey, Serra chose Juan Evangelista, an Indian he had baptized a few years earlier. On October 20th, the return to Mexico began under the patronage of Our Lady of Guadalupe, "the sovereign Queen of Angels and the Mother of Navigators." It was the beginning of a journey that would alter the course of California's history.

As Serra sailed southward along the coast, he reviewed his time in Alta California. Five missions had been founded, even though some of them were still in a precarious state. The *Presidente* felt that unless the laws were enforced and a change in personalities was made, the greatly desired mission progress would never be attained.

Case for the Friars

BY the time Fray Junípero Serra left San Diego, it had become evident in California, Mexico and even in Spain itself that the strained relations between the military and religious in that faraway province had resulted in an embarrassing and dangerous impasse.

Governor Pedro Fages was young, gruff, rigid and new to America. He was inexperienced in governing a mission territory. Zealous in the service of the king and in upholding the dignity of the military profession, he was a disciplinarian whose methods, instead of improving his men, often made them worse.

For his part, Serra was zealous, dynamic and seasoned in mission experience. Position and preferment he voluntarily cast aside. A naturally impatient man, the *Presidente* was frustrated by imperfect conditions.

Serra felt that conversions would not be unnecessarily delayed if the agencies of conquest were really interested in souls. Optimistic, courageous and willing to take chances, Serra had great faith in the providence of God. Delays, vexations and disappointments weighed heavily on him.

Some of the soldiers were lazy, inept, disorderly and scandalous. The lack of food supplies, sufficient mules and personnel and of Christianized Indians as helpers prevented a more rapid development of the missions.

While Galvez had determined the salient features of the conquest and its manner of operation thereafter, too much was left to individual caprice, especially with the rapid change of personnel in high places. Antonio Maria Bucareli recognized the problems in California and on March 18, 1772, he suggested to Fages that he, "preserve harmony with the missionary Fathers and let them freely perform their apostolic work, assisting them with all means possible so that they may attain, as soon as possible, the reduction of those to whom they desire to preach."

Disharmony between the agencies of conquest was apparent at all levels of the governmental hierarchy. And, at that psychological moment, Serra decided that the atmosphere could be cleared only by a personal conference. This turned the tide. His decision to go to Mexico was one of the wisest of his life.

There is no doubt that the core of the entire California enterprise was the establishment of missions for the conversion and civilization of the Indians, even though a political consideration had been the occasion of effecting the conquest. The Christianization process was to be implemented by tried missionary methods; the friars became the principal agents of the peaceful conquest. Their rule over the Indians was to be complete, except in certain criminal matters.

"What soldiers are closer to the arrows than we?" wrote Serra in 1773. The development of the soil, the furtherance of animal husbandry, the teaching of the trades, the development of the arts, the introduction of European social and domestic habits, the gradual formation of towns, the propagation of religion and morality, all of this was the work of the missionary. For these ends, the government provided wide jurisdiction and often generous help, for his labors were recognized as a benefit to the state as well as to the Church.

What Serra was seeking in Mexico City was not so much new laws and methods, but rather a return to the smoother, non confrontational approach used so successfully in the Sierra Gorda, Texas and other areas.

The Presidente *and* the Viceroy

FRAY Junípero Serra and his traveling companions reached the Franciscan college at Mexico City on February 6, 1773. Shortly thereafter, he sought a personal interview with Viceroy Antonio Bucareli at the Palacio Nacional, just east of the *zocalo.*

Though still suffering from a near-fatal fever contracted enroute, the little man from Mallorca, who was the spearhead of the spiritual conquest in the king's most recently acquired territory, was to deal directly with the *alter ego* of Charles III. Bucareli received Serra cordially and listened with interest to what he had to say. The viceroy had been briefed beforehand by letters which Serra had sent to his college from Tepic.

Bucareli told Serra to put all his petitions in writing and to present them formally to the court. Impressed with Serra's zeal and his knowledge of affairs, the viceroy told him he would cooperate in any way possible.

Serra was heartened over the meeting, for Bucareli's attitude was one of warmhearted interest. He had obtained a friend at court of whom none was higher. Once more Serra had gone forward and not turned back. The gate of the viceregal palace was a gate of victory for Serra and all of California.

Upon returning to San Fernando College, Serra began writing his report about the problems and needs of Alta California. The *representación* was finished and signed on March 13th. It was an interesting document and it formed the basis for the first significant legislation for early California, legislation that would affect Indians, soldiers, military commanders, naval men, post office officials, missionaries, colonists, the college, the palace and the Council of the Indies in Spain.

The twenty-two points in the report covered practically every phase of activity about the missionary enterprise. Serra devoted the greatest amount of space to the military governor of Monterey and why he should be replaced. Unless Pedro Fages were removed from office, the development of the missions would be impaired. Serra suggested Jose Francisco Ortega as a replacement, noting that "insofar as I have observed, in commanding soldiers he is firm without being offensive, is prudent and judicious."

To better satisfy the soldiers, Serra suggested that a warehouse be built for them, that the price of goods be regulated, and their annual pay increased. He suggested, furthermore, the recruitment of married soldiers. Each mission was to have a *majordomo,* or missionary soldier, who would supervise, under the *padre,* the manual and economic duties at the missions as had been done in Baja California.

Serra asked that the "immemorial custom" be restored in California whereby the management, command, punishment and education of the baptized Indians and those ready to receive baptism remain under the friars exclusively. Only crimes of blood were to be reserved to the military. All punishments then would be inflicted only after prior consultation with the missionary in charge.

The *Presidente's* report covered many other aspects of the missionary program in Alta California. In concluding his *representación,* Serra promised to abide scrupulously by the decisions of the government.

The document is, in many ways, a remarkable expose of needs and difficulties, frankly expressed. Serra made definite, concrete proposals and showed himself a man of practical affairs. He sought legislation that covered every possible mission relationship and, in so doing, he became the sponsor of the first body of laws to govern early California.

Government Responds
to Serra

AFTER receiving Fray Junípero Serra's *representación,* Viceroy Bucareli called a meeting of the viceregal council to consider the points spelled out by the *Presidente.* On May 13, Serra was informed that his proposals had been mostly approved. Serra considered that he had obtained everything he had asked for; still more important, he had gained a powerful and benevolent friend at court who would be useful and cooperative in the years to come.

The most significant of the council's grants to Serra was that which stated that "the government, control and education of the baptized Indians should belong exclusively to the missionaries." The friars were to have a parental relationship with the Indians in economic affairs, in correction and in education.

Pedro Fages was removed from office, to be replaced by Fernando Rivera de Moncada. The overland expeditions were to be undertaken, immoral soldiers were to be removed upon the request of a missionary, prices would be regulated and weights standardized. The *padres'* mail would come in separate packets and their official correspondence would enjoy governmental frankage. A doctor, blacksmiths, carpenters, bells and vestments would be provided.

Serra's request for a hundred soldiers was considered excessive and he was asked to submit further reasons for that and other needs to the council. Another session of the viceregal body was called to consider everything that had been negotiated since the first meeting.

In a note to his nephew, Serra said that "His Excellency has attended to all my requests and has granted as much as I have asked for. Through this, I hope, with God's help, a speedy and enlarged expansion of our holy Faith and of the dominions of our Catholic Monarch."

Serra's busy months in Mexico City were coming to a close. He had taken care of a great variety of business items. Among other things, he had one of the more famous painters of the time, Joseph

Paez, to do oil paintings of the patron saints of the California missions so far established.

When the *Presidente* was ready to leave for California, the College of San Fernando took particularly good care of him, for there were misgivings as to whether he would reach his destination. The guardian gave him as companion Fray Pablo de Mugartegui who, at the same time, was to serve as chaplain of a new frigate bound for California waters. Serra set out on his journey in September of 1773.

Before leaving, Serra asked permission to do what he had done twenty-four years earlier when he left Palma, namely, to perform an act of humility and of esteem toward all his brethren assembled in community. He received permission to kiss the feet of all, from first to last, begging pardon for all the faults he might have committed.

Serra asked his brethren to commend him to God for they would never see his face again. "In California is my life," he had once written, "and God willing, there I hope to die." His biographer later wrote that "he touched the hearts of all in such a way that they shed copious tears. They were edified at his great humility and fervor in undertaking so long a journey at an advanced age and in such poor health that he was almost unable to stand."

He was off again, but not before writing his nephew to report that "I am restored to health and am brought back . . . and feel ready to set out on my journey back to that vineyard of the Lord."

Home to Carmel

AFTER completing his affairs in Mexico City, Serra, Fray Pablo Mugartegui and the Indian Juan Evangelista set out for California. They arrived at San Diego after a forty day voyage, on March 13, 1774. Serra found the *padres* at San Diego Mission in good health and working hard. Spiritually the foundation had prospered and in economic statistics the mission could show a crop of wheat, an increase in cattle and milk in abundance.

The *Presidente* heard much of what had transpired in his absence. California had almost succumbed to famine, but despite the shortage of food, progress had been made. Like other missions, San Diego had problems. The first year, flood waters destroyed the crop. The second year, when seeds were planted further away from the river banks, water was scarce and the crop perished.

It was then that it was decided that an inland valley location would prove a better site and Serra authorized the change. The new location proved better for reasons other than agricultural too.

Serra had a great deal to tell his confreres of his successful dealing with the viceroy. He was able to promise a better future because Bucareli had taken a personal interest in the missions.

On March 22nd, a surprise expedition arrived at San Gabriel in the person of Juan Bautista de Anza, Fray Francisco Garces and others. The incredible had happened. The mission had been reached overland from Sonora. Bucareli had asked Serra about the feasibility of the route and the *Presidente* recognized its value and optimistically endorsed it.

Serra left San Diego on April 6th. The forty leagues to San Gabriel took six days, longer than usual because of the heavy rains and mud along the road. On the 23rd, Serra, Juan Evangelista and several others set out for San Luis Obispo. Enroute he met Anza. The two great men spoke of mighty plans for the future. Father Maynard Geiger thought the spot of that meeting should be commemorated by a plaque which might read: "Here on April

28, 1774, Anza and Serra, builders of an empire, met and conferred about the California-to-be."

After a brief respite at San Luis Obispo, Serra proceeded on north to San Antonio. Then on to Monterey and Carmel. Fray Francisco Palou related that Serra's arrival caused an outbreak of joy on the part of everyone because of the success he had achieved.

Serra wrote to the viceroy that "after so many journeys by land and sea, I am here well and safe in the mission of Monterey so greatly favored by Your Excellency. Now all the land, heretofore so melancholy and miserable, is rejoicing because of the abundant provisions and most fitting measures with which Your Excellency has consoled us."

The supply ship had arrived too and "all past sufferings were turned into joy, declared Serra. Chocolate and tortillas, ham and flour, oil and wine were there for all. And Juan Evangelista was back among his people with stories of what he had seen and heard in a distant land.

Serra had indeed reason for gratitude to the viceroy. And he expressed it in another letter: "If the opinion of many persons is true that conservation is no less a benefit than creation, these provinces ought not to be less obligated, nor consider themselves less indebted to the piety and zeal of Your Excellency than to those who began the colonization and spiritual conquest."

Serra had never looked for smooth sailing on rough seas or smiling fields on desert terrain. He expected to meet hardships and difficulties, but he was also determined that they would not needlessly remain forever.

Apostolate in Action

FERNANDO Rivera arrived at Monterey on May 23, 1774, to assume the commandancy from Pedro Fages. Fray Junípero Serra and Rivera were old acquaintances, having first met in Baja California in 1768. It was a transition that brought fresh hope to the frontier.

Serra now settled into the daily routine of life along the waters of Carmel Bay. He took special interest in the baptisms at San Carlos. By August 24th, two hundred and forty-five persons had been christened, seventy-two of them children over eight years of age.

The *Presidente's* great hope for the future was the children. He noted that "the spectacle of seeing a hundred young children of about the same age praying and answering individually all the questions asked on Christian doctrine, hearing them sing, seeing them going about clothed, playing happily . . . is, indeed, something moving, a thing for which God is to be thanked."

Harvest time for 1774 was approaching and Serra could tell the viceroy that the Indians of Carmel Valley, with a few Baja California natives working among them, were applying themselves in field, orchard and woodland. The collected grain was brought to the mission storehouse from which it was rationed daily to the converts and catechumens. While the harvest was in progress, large schools of sardines appeared in Carmel Bay and it was too good an opportunity for the Indians to miss. After all, they had been fishermen long before they had become farmers.

So a compromise was arranged. The Indians harvested in the morning and fished in the afternoon, keeping up the double occupation for twenty days. The fish were dried in the sun.

Juan Evangelista, the faithful companion of Serra during the long journey to Mexico City, wanted to send the viceroy a present in the name of his parents. Serra encouraged the idea and a barrel of dried sardines was dispatched to Antonio Bucareli. The viceroy received the gift, was impressed and acknowledged the kindness of Juan.

On one of the Sundays during the harvest season, the white sands of Carmel Bay presented a picturesque spectacle. It was a day of rest. The Indians searched the rocks looking for birds that lived on sardines. Describing the scene to Bucareli, Serra said the groups of picnickers looked like gatherings of *rancherías;* "it was like sitting in a beautiful theatre."

That summer, the *Santiago* was sailing north along the coast. The expedition's objective was to reach the sixtieth parallel, but it succeeded in getting only as far as the fifty-fifth. The standard of the cross was placed on Queen Charlotte Island, now part of Canada. Using the language of the naval men in describing the voyage, Serra spoke of the *padres* aboard the ship as "going to Russia." They were indeed in the sphere of Russian influence.

Juan Evangelista married, on December 2, 1775, Thomasa Maria of the *ranchería* of Ichxenta, with Fray Junípero Serra witnessing the ceremony. Their married life was short for Thomasa was buried on August 1, 1778 and Juan followed her to the grave nine days afterward.

Serra kept himself busy at Carmel. Every phase of mission life called for his time and attention. The Indians, soldiers, colonists, crops, buildings, mules, ships from San Blas, his own missionaries, the military governor, the viceroy—all these matters fell under his guidance in differing ways.

The *Presidente* complained that his life was being consumed in writing letters. He was becoming more of a scribe than he should. But, as *Presidente,* "the solicitude of all the churches" came under his care and this called for the frequent use of quill and paper.

Problems along
El Camino Real

FOR Fray Junípero Serra, the period from March, 1773 to
May, 1774 was a time of joy, progress and triumph. His
letters were full of warm gratitude, ebullient optimism and
bright hopes. The California enterprise was going well.

But soon minor problems began to surface. The discontent was
occasioned by Fernando de Rivera, the new commander, whom
from the beginning Serra considered a roadblock to the program
so harmoniously projected by the viceroy. Serra lacked enthusiasm
for Rivera from the very moment he had heard of his appointment
and now at Monterey he became convinced that he had not been
in error when he judged that he could never expect much cooperation from the commander.

Jose de Galvez too had his misgivings about Rivera as a military
leader, as well as about his willingness to take the initiative. Rivera
had received the same instructions as Serra and had copies of the
same documents prepared by the viceregal government. However,
government in practice is one thing, in theory is another.

No matter what had been decreed in Spain or Mexico, ultimate
success in California depended upon the cooperation of the
commander and the Franciscan *Presidente*. The sad fact is that
despite the viceroy's generosity, both Serra and Rivera did at times
lack the necessary wherewithal to forge ahead, due mostly to the
great distance between California and its sources of supply.

Serra was certainly the greatest enthusiast for the prosecution
of the California conquest. Through all negotiations he always
appeared as the incurable optimist. His zeal and sincerity had won
over Antonio Bucareli. But Serra was realistic enough to realize
that not everyone shared his goals and methods.

The *Presidente* felt that after five years of operation, the Alta
California missions were in as good shape as those of Peninsular
California and, of course, his plans were to perfect them. He was

forever trying to keep lighted the three fires he had enkindled: at Monterey, at the palace and at the college.

Despite the fact that Serra had gone to Mexico principally to have Pedro Fages removed and to have substituted for him a successor who would work with him harmoniously, that purpose was not attained with the appointment of Rivera. Disputes and misunderstandings were almost continuous. That anything was accomplished at all is nothing short of a miracle.

Serra's aim was to found as many missions as possible for the prime objective of converting the Indians, as is plain from reading his numerous and pleading letters. He especially wanted to see San Buenaventura, so long delayed, become a reality. His idea was to build ten or eleven missions in his lifetime and thus have a ladder with conveniently placed rungs. (He always referred to the series of missions as a ladder, each one a rung, something one climbed up and down with no little labor).

Sometime prior to mid 1774, Serra proposed to Rivera the founding of San Buenaventura. He later wrote that his request was refused with "such reasoning" that if a hundred additional soldiers were added to the *presidios*, Rivera would still offer the same negative objections.

The *Presidente* was more than willing to take the plunge. He felt that without taking a calculated risk, nothing would be accomplished. He recalled that the reason for Spain's presence in California was to convert and civilize the Indians. He could see no reason for delay when there was a probability of success. It was a clash between Rivera's "military prudence" and Serra's "spiritual imprudence."

But Serra was a pragmatist. After broaching the subject in a humble way, pleading for the cause that was close to his heart, he let the matter drop. But he never for a moment doubted that eventually he would get his way. And he did.

Complexities
of Mission Life

F RAY Junípero Serra's zeal and determination to establish
more missions continued unabated into 1775. He still wanted
four missions to be founded between Monterey and San
Diego as a "ladder" for better communications. Two of these,
San Buenaventura and Santa Clara, should be located along the
populous Santa Barbara channel. At the very least, San Buenaventura should be located there. That particular mission was Serra's
great desire, yet, he wrote, "despite all I have done to have it
established, I have not been able to see it realized."

Word arrived at Monterey in June of 1775, ordering the
establishment of two missions and a *presidio* in the San Francisco
area. Captain Juan Bautista de Anza was coming for that purpose
with soldiers, settlers and supplies. The news "filled me with joy,"
Serra told the viceroy by letter.

The *Presidente* continued to urge the establishment of a mission
along the Santa Barbara Channel. He described the passage as
dangerous and the natives as numerous and spirited. With Pedro
Fages, he had witnessed an encounter with them at the Rincon in
1772, and recently there had been a battle at Dos Pueblos where
the Indians attacked the Monterey pack train. Volleys of Spanish
bullets answered the flying arrows of the Indians.

The baptismal register of San Carlos Mission between May 11,
1774 and the end of 1775 does not merely record baptisms. Serra
added many interesting notes which help reconstruct not only the
spiritual activity but the general history and statistics of the area.
Of the one hundred and ninety-four baptisms administered from
Serra's return from Mexico until the end of 1775, he personally
performed one hundred and seventy-one. As a matter of fact,
Serra baptized the very first one who was prepared.

Most of the Indian infants as well as the adults came from the
towns of the Carmel Valley—San Francisco, Santa Teresa, San
Miguel, San Carlos, San Jose and other smaller places. Of

particular interest is entry no. 350, which shows Serra was deep in the Santa Lucia mountain country, inland from Big Sur:

> On May 9, 1775, in the *ranchería* of Xasauan in the *sierra* about ten leagues from this Mission of San Carlos de Monterey, toward the east, I baptized privately an adult about ninety years of age in danger of death, married, and who is captain of the Excelen territory and its *rancherías,* called Pachhepas, and I gave him the name Miguel Gregorio. The greater part of the natives of both sexes of that *ranchería* were present at the baptism and they gave signs of happiness on seeing their new chief now a Christian and offered good hope of imitating him. I sign, giving testimony thereto, Fray Junípero Serra.

Besides the naval men whom Serra honored from time-to-time with sponsorship of those to be baptized, he frequently employed the soldiers, the servants, the skilled workmen and their wives to act as sponsors. Thus can be seen the people whom the *Presidente* had brought to California on the *Santiago* frequently mentioned in the Carmel register book. Conspicuously absent from the register is the name of Fernando Rivera y Moncada.

Serra's difficulties with the commander were fairly well pinpointed by his biographer who put it this way: When Serra proposed something, Rivera refused to accede; after delaying a month or so, he would usually do what was requested. Then (and now), such human tactics were annoying, to say the least.

Martyrdom at San Diego

THE Franciscans were especially lavish in bestowing their blood and virtue on the Church in California. Prominently etched onto the Golden State's martyrology are the names of six outstanding friars whose testimony for Christ is forever a monument to Christian endurance and bravery.

Fray Luis Jayme (1740–1775), a native of the tranquil farming village of San Juan de Mallorca, was immensely pleased when the *Presidente* of the California Missions appointed him to what would be his first and last assignment, San Diego de Alcalá. A clever and talented friar, Jayme's earliest efforts at San Diego were devoted to mastering the complexities of the local native language. Once he had gained a facility with its vocabulary, he was able to compile a Christian catechism.

The extreme scarcity of water, combined with the proximity of the military personnel, induced Fray Luis to ask for and receive permission to move the mission from its original site, atop Presidio Hill, to the valley where it is presently situated.

The new location proved eminently more practical. Almost immediately there was a notable upsurge in the number of conversions which by 1775, numbered 431. Such success obviously infuriated the devil who seems to have held the natives at San Diego in bondage during aboriginal times. In any event, a plan was hatched by a handful of pagan sorcerers and others to rid the area of all traces of Hispanic influence.

At about 1:30, on the brilliantly-lit night of November 4, 1775, 600 or more warriors from some forty *rancherías* silently crept into the mission compound. After quietly plundering the chapel, they set fire to the other buildings. The crackling of flames soon awakened the two missionaries, the guards and the Christian neophytes.

Instead of running for shelter, Fray Luis Jayme resolutely walked toward the howling band of natives, uttering the traditional Franciscan greeting: *"Amar a Dios, hijo"*. In a frenzied orgy of cruelty, the Indians seized him, stripped off his garments, shot eighteen arrows into his body and then pulverized his face with clubs and stones.

The attack on the mission was only terminated when a well-aimed shot from a musket unnerved the Indians and caused them to flee in panic. Early next morning, the body of the thirty-five year old missionary was recovered in the dry bed of a nearby creek. His face was so disfigured that he could only be recognized by the whiteness of his flesh under a thick crust of congealed blood.

The friar's mangled body was initially buried in the *presidio* chapel. When the new church at the mission was completed, it was re-interred in the sanctuary. There it rested until November 12, 1813, when it was transferred to the third and final church.

Reaction of Fray Junípero Serra to the news of his confrere's death speaks volumes about the attitude of the early friars. Far from being saddened or disappointed the *Presidente* said: "Thanks be to God; now that the terrain has been watered by blood, the conversion of the San Diego Indians will take place." It was a paraphrase of Tertullian's *sanguis, semen Christianorum* which freely translates says that "the blood of martyrs is the seed of the Church."

Immediately Serra wrote to Bucareli, reminding the Viceroy that he had earlier asked "that in case the Indians, whether pagans or Christians would kill me, they should be pardoned." He wanted that request renewed. In addition he wanted "to see a formal decree from Your Excellency for me and the other religious, present and future, and it will give me special consolation to have it in my hands during the years that God may deign to add to my life."

Thus would be avoided the mistakes of San Saba (in the Texas missions) where reprisals against the Indians had totally stalled the missionary work among them. Serra sadly recalled that "there in San Saba the soldiers are still in their *presidios* and the Indians in their paganism."

A Pause for Reflection

DURING 1776, a significant year in American history when political and social experiments were being tested on both the Atlantic and Pacific coasts, the Juan Bautista de Anza expedition marched north through the mission territory of Alta California and occasioned a survey of the development up to that time.

The mission system in California was only seven years old in 1776. For the moment, San Juan Capistrano did not exist. San Diego lay in ruins, awaiting resurrection; because of its poor resources for agriculture, many of its converted Indians still lived in their *rancherías* and were often Christian in name only. San Luis Obispo, San Antonio, San Carlos and San Gabriel were relatively prosperous.

Though the early days at San Gabriel had been difficult, by 1776 the mission was flourishing. It was built in the midst of broad plains; abundant water was at hand; pasture was plentiful; forests of live oaks provided timber for firewood and building. The mission had horses, cows, pigs, sheep and chickens.

In his diary, Fray Pedro Font says that the cows were fat, the milk rich and the mutton finer than any he had ever tasted. Another friar had called San Gabriel the Promised Land and Font echoed him. In 1776, all roads led to San Gabriel; southeast the overland route was now open all the way to Mexico City; north to San Francisco; south to San Diego and Baja California. This was the gateway to coastal California.

The buildings at San Gabriel were still rather primitive. Some were made of adobe, but most were built of logs and tule. The friars lived in a long shed where grain was also stored. The church was a rectangular edifice. Eight soldiers lived in the guardhouse. About five hundred Indians resided in native huts close to the mission, an aqueduct running between their homes and the mission.

The mission system which Font found in operation at San Gabriel was the pattern upon which all the other missions were based, a system begun in Texas, followed in the Sierra Gorda and then transmitted to Alta California. Attracted to the missions by the *padres,* the Indians lived as catechumens until they were ready for baptism. During this period, they were taught the elements of the Catholic faith, were fed and clothed, taught to work and to follow the routine of mission life.

If, after several months they had learned the catechism and desired to become Christians, they were baptized. Thereafter they were required to live permanently at the mission and to learn to live a fuller Christian life in the pattern of Spanish culture. Converts were given permission to visit their pagan relatives for a few days at a time; it gave the Indian a change of routine and the mission Indians often brought more of their relatives and friends to the mission. Runaways who had been baptized were sought out and returned to the mission.

After sunrise, the Indians assembled at the sound of the bell, assisted at Mass, and recited with the *padre* the *doctrina* a compendium of Christian doctrine and prayers. At the conclusion, the *Alabado* was sung. Breakfast, preceded by grace, consisted of *atole* (porridge). Afterwards, the morning's labors were assigned, each Indian going to his work under the supervision of a *padre* who often worked alongside. At noon, the Indians ate their *pozole* (a stew of barley, beans and other ingredients) in common. A short period of labor in the afternoon was concluded with the Indians assembling again to recite the *doctrina*.

This was the California of 1776.

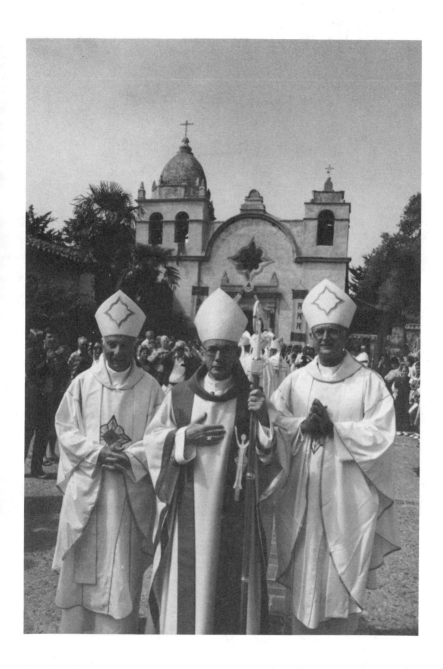

Timothy Cardinal Manning, Archbishop Pio Laghi (Papal Pro-Nuncio) and Bishop Thaddeus Shubsda gather with the California hierarchy at Carmel to celebrate the 200th anniversary of Fray Junípero Serra's demise.

APOSTLE
OF CALIFORNIA

VOL. 5; No. 3   QUARTERLY BULLETIN   JANUARY, 1948

for the Cause of Fr Junipero Serra

PADRE SERRA----LINGUIST

FOREIGN LANGUAGES are hard for most people to learn. Padre Serra was no exception. From Carmel Mission in 1772, he wrote to his friend, Fr. Francisco Palou, "In my opinion, the fact that not everyone here has yet been converted to christianity, is due simply to our ignorance of their language. This difficulty in learning a language, is nothing new to me. I have always thought that my sins made me unworthy of such a favor."—How many languages did he probably know?

HIS STUDIES for the priesthood had required Padre Serra to learn a good deal of Greek and Hebrew, and in working for his degree as Doctor of Sacred Theology, he must have gone into these languages more deeply than the ordinary student. His Province of Mallorca was strongly under the influence of the Blessed Raymond Lull, martyred by the Mohammedans of North Africa. Blessed Raymond had founded a college for the study of Arabic and other oriental languages; he was buried in the church of San Francisco at Palma, where Padre Serra lived. Whether all this influenced the young Serra to include oriental languages in his own studies, is another interesting question, as yet unanswered. His great knowledge of Sacred Scripture, might lend weight to this possibility.

LATIN, of course, he knew well. Over eleven hundred pages of his lectures on philosophy, delivered in Latin to the students in Palma, have been gathered for the Cause. He knew and used not only the language of the Church, a Latin enriched by the truths of divine revelation, and colored by the nationality and personality of the saintly scholars of eastern and western Europe and northern Africa. Into his writings and lectures,

Padre Serra could weave quotations from Virgil, Terrence, Seneca, Quintilian, Lucretius, etc. He knew the Latin classics well.

MALLORCAN CHILDREN today grow up speaking both Spanish and Mallorcan. The latter is a dialect, similar to the Catalonian, to French, and somewhat to Portuguese. Padre Serra must have had the same start in life. Four sermons—all that is known of his brilliant productions as a pulpit orator—have been found in his native Mallorcan. Once he came to the New World, he seems never to have written in that dialect again, using the Castilian exclusively.

HIS VOYAGE TO AMERICA in 1749 was begun on an English ship· Fr. Palou writes, "During the two weeks that the voyage lasted till we reached Malaga, the captain did not leave us in peace, because he wished continually to argue and dispute with us about dogmas. He did not know any other language except English, save for a little Portuguese, in which he could barely make himself understood, but he presented his arguments in the latter." —Clearly, then, Padre Serra did not know English. Still, in view of the great development of English trade and travel during the eighteenth century, he might well have learned something of it, while he lived in the seaport of Palma.

INDIAN LANGUAGES OR DIALECTS were to make his work difficult during the second half of his life, from thirty-six to seventy, when the memory is naturally less quick and retentive. But in the Sierra Gorda of Mexico, he learned the Pame dialect of his Indians of Jalpan, and translated into it the catechism and various prayers. These writings, it seems, have been irretrievably lost.

The Apostle of California *was the official organ for the Cause of Fray Junípero Serra between 1943 and 1958. It kept the memory of Serra alive in areas untouched by books and other ephemeral publications.*

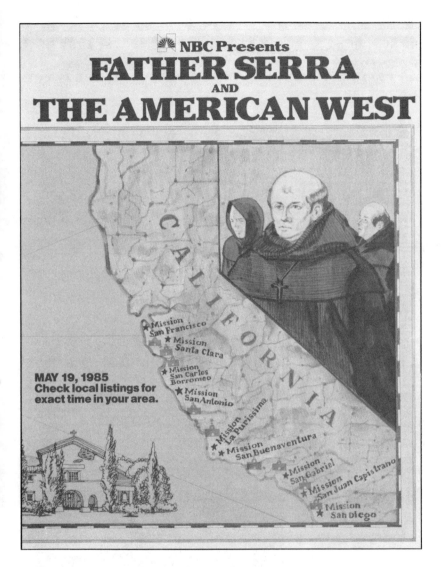

Advertisement issued by the National Broadcasting Corporation for a "special" on Fray Junípero Serra, 1985.

THE 250ᵀᴴ ANIVERSARY OF FRAY JUNIPERO SERRA

PRESIDENT KENNEDY: «THESE CELEBRATIONS ARE A FITTING REMINDER OF OUR SPANISH HERITAGE»

THIS message from the President of the United States was read at the closing of the acts held to marg the 250th Anniversary of the birth of Fray Junipero Serra at Petra (Majorca).

«I send best wishes to the people of Spain and particularly to those gathered in Majorca on the occasion of the 250th Anniversary of the birth of Father Junipero Serra the founder of California. These celebrations are a fitting reminder of our Spanish heritage whose virtues were exemplified in the piety, courage and vision of Father Serra.—John F. Kennedy.»

At the same act, the Bishop of Majorca Dr. Enciso read messages from Cardinal Larraona and Cardinal Cicognani, the Vatican Secretary of State. Texts are as follows:

«The Vatican, 1st of June. 6 p. m. Unavoidably absent splendid fiestas commemorating great Apostle California, with you in spirit send cordial best wishes and letter to follow for Secretary of State Office. Offer Minister greetings and warmest hopes success commemorative acts. Sincerely, Cardinal Larraona.»

«The Holy Father, who feels himself, in these days of meditation and prayer, amid his sufferings and sacrifice, more intimately united to all the faithful of the world, wishes Your Eminence to convey his paternal affection to those most dearly beloved sons in Majorca, to the most excellent Franciscan Family, to all those in Spain and America, and in particular the ecclesiastical and civil authorities —who are now gathered on the native soil of the illustrious Missionary, to whom he sends a special apostolic blessing which Your Eminence is authorized to bestow on the customary conditions — Cardinal Cicognani.»

In his speech, the Chief Justice of the United States Supreme Court, Justice Earl Warren said:

«Without any question at all, it is a moving experience for a Californian to visit Petra and the house of Fr. Junipero Serra in circumstances like these, and I am very grateful to the Spanish Government for having invited me to take part in these ceremonies.

«Many speeches have been made and much has been said during the last few days about the life of Fr. Serra. More will be said during the days that follow this anniversary of his birth. We have heard words from a famous historian, from distinguished members of the Government, from the clergy and great experts on the life of Fr. Serra. It is difficult to tell you anything new about him, as Majorcans, but it is always good to recall the deeds of a great man who has influenced the lives of generations, even though what I say may have been said before, and undoubtedly, said better. I speak to you today chiefly as a Californian, whose State has been especially enriched thanks to the fact that Fr. Serra passed through it and because the lives of my wife and my children have, like my own, been especially benefited by this.

«When the good people of this Island and the Spanish Government honor his 250th anniversary at the spot where he came into the world in this great Majorca, they honor Spaniards and Americans. Fr. Junipero Serra belongs equally to you and to us. It was here that he was born and dedicated his life to God and to Humanity. It was in California where his deeds bore fruit after a long life of dedication, sacrifice, courage and achievements. You honor his birthplace. In California we honor the place where his remains rest in peace. Both places are little villages of humble appearance. Here there is a poor but holy house. In California there is a humble house of prayer. One of the missionary chain he founded; perhaps his favorite. At any rate, one he very much loved. This mission is San Carlos in the little seashore town of Carmel, situated in a place similar to those that inspired him in

The Chief Justice of the United States Supreme Court, Justice Earl Warren and the Deputy Governor of California Mr. Anderson together with the Spanish Minister of Information and Tourism Sr. Fraga Iribarne at one of the acts held at Petra

Special Souvenir broadside issued at Petra de Mallorca, 1963.

A bi-lingual edition of this comic book was issued in the fall of 1987 by Franciscan Communications of Los Angeles. Written by Roy Gasnick, O.F.M., it was partially sponsored by the Serra International Foundation.

This letter from Fray Junípero Serra to Fray Fermin Francisco de Lasuen was written from San Buenaventura Mission on March 31, 1782. It is here produced from the Santa Barbara Mission Archives.

Postcard depictions of Fray Junípero Serra.

The Postmaster General

invites you to a ceremony dedicating the

Junipero Serra Airmail Stamp

Copper Room

San Diego Convention and Performing Arts Center

202 C Street

San Diego, California

10:30 a.m., Thursday, August 22, 1985

JUNIPERO SERRA
FRANCISCAN MISSIONARY

US AIRMAIL 44¢

San Carlos Borromeo de Carmelo

FIRST DAY COVER

Rotary Station
August 23, 1985
Mission Hills, Ca. 91345

Msgr. Francis J. Weber
San Fernando Mission
15151 San Fernando Mission Bl.
Mission Hills, California
91345

Souvenir Cachet signed by the Postmaster General for issuance of commemorative stamp honoring Fray Junípero Serra.

Serra and Washington

THE handsomely-fashioned bronze likeness of Fray Junípero Serra, located in the Statuary Hall of the nation's capitol, appropriately faces the one depicting George Washington. Surely there was something more than coincidence in the proximity of the two great pioneers, one the "Father of his Country," the other a "Father" of his Church.

George Washington (1732–1799) and Junípero Serra (1713–1784) were contemporaries in ideals as well as in time. They worked for a common cause, each in his own sphere.

In 1776, the year associated with the Declaration of Independence, Fray Junípero Serra established the Mission of San Francisco beside the Golden Gate. By the time of his death, less than a decade later, a new nation had been born. While George Washington and his patriots fought for independence, Fray Junípero introduced Christian civilization into an area that would eventually join forces as the thirty-first member of the American commonwealth.

At the time there was little more than a vast wilderness and a few French colonies between the Atlantic and Pacific oceans. Chances are that Washington gave very little thought to California.

When Spain entered the war with the English, the "perfidious heretics," Serra's sentiments identified immediately with those of Washington. He asked his fellow missionaries, in 1780, to be "most attentive in begging God to grant success to this public cause which is so favorable to our holy Catholic and Roman Church." Personality-wise, Washington and Serra were resourceful innovators, stern disciplinarians and exemplary pacesetters, the one dedicated to his people in the civil realm, the other to serving them in the religious sphere. Both men fit into the category of "charismatic" leaders. Washington and Serra fulfilled their particular commissions, not alone by mandate, but rather by virtue of dynamic personalities which instilled an incredible loyalty and devotion among their respective peoples.

Though George Washington and Junípero Serra differed considerably in their religious convictions, secular vocations and human endowments, the qualities they shared are exceedingly more impressive than the ones they differed in. "Great places make great men," Oliver Wendell Holmes once observed. Washington and Serra, each in his own way, proved the enduring wisdom of Holmes' aphorism.

As widely divergent as were their concepts about God, George Washington and Junípero Serra would surely have identified their sentiments in that beautiful prayer subsequently composed by John Henry Newman:

God created me to do Him some definite service; He has committed some work to me which He has not committed to another. I have my mission—I may never know it in this life, but I shall be told it in the next. I am a link in a chain, a bond of connection between persons. He has not created me for naught. I shall do good; I shall do His work. I shall be an angel of peace, a preacher of truth in my own place, while not intending it—if I do but keep His Commandments. Therefore will I trust Him. Whatever, wherever I am. I can never be thrown away. If I am in sickness, my sickness may serve Him: in perplexity, my perplexity may serve Him; in sorrow, my sorrow may serve Him. He does nothing in vain. He knows what He is about. He may take away my friends; He may throw me among strangers. He may make me feel desolate, make my spirits sink, hide my future from me—still He knows what He is about.

The Presidente *Moves On*

IN mid 1776, Fray Junípero Serra sailed south to the desecrated San Diego where he hoped to formally re-establish the mission. Since it was the dry season of the year, favorable to building, he hoped to finish the work before the rains began.

Unfortunately Fernando de Rivera, who was also at San Diego, had the work suspended when word reached him that the Indians were regrouping for another attack on the mission. Though it was likely only a rumor, he decided it would be better to halt reconstruction, at least temporarily.

There were also economic problems at San Diego. The mission had no food of its own for the *padres* and the neophytes except the surviving cattle. Rations for the handful of sailors, soldiers and friars were sparse, to say the least.

Since he was thwarted in his attempt to rebuild the mission, Serra found other ways to occupy himself at San Diego. He gathered and examined the church goods ruined by the fire, among them a silver chalice with its paten and spoon. He shipped them back to San Fernando College for repair or replacement. Many of the mission's articles were still in the hands of the Indians who participated in the destruction of the buildings.

On September 16, 1776, Serra inscribed a new baptismal register, writing therein a concise history of the early days at San Diego in 1769. He later entered the names of the sixteen persons who had been baptized there. Other names were added later, as the friars could recall them.

One item that Serra salvaged was the complete catechism in the Diegueño language which had been composed by Fray Luis Jayme. During his stay in San Diego, Serra observed that in each village there was an Indian religious instructor and many catechists. A large number of youngsters knew how to serve Mass and a soprano choir sang the *Asperges* and other music "to perfection." In September, military reinforcements arrived at San Diego, causing great rejoicing at the *presidio*. Serra had the bells rung in honor of the event and, on the feast of Saint Michael, he sang a High Mass "for the health and wellbeing" of the viceroy.

Serra received three letters from Bucareli which the soldiers delivered. The first stated that the royal treasury would willingly bear the expenses of delivering supplies by land and sea for the missions to be founded in the San Francisco area. The second said that twenty-five additional soldiers were being sent to California to reinforce the mission guards.

The third letter, dated April 3, 1776, ordered that the Indians guilty of the November massacre and fire be treated with kindness and pardoned, and that Missions San Diego and San Juan Capistrano were to be re-established. Serra passed along the information about clemency for the Indians to Rivera and thus prevented any further action being taken against them. Rivera gave orders to proceed with work at the two sites. He addressed the soldiers, urging obedience in assisting with the many chores that were inseparable from founding a mission.

The *Presidente* wrote to the viceroy, telling him of the "pleasure, happiness and consolation" that had resulted from his directives. He assured Bucareli that "we shall pursue with all our strength the work we have begun."

Once more fired with zeal and energy, Fray Junípero Serra was now ready to go forward again.

The Ball Begins Rolling

FRAY Junípero Serra supervised the rebuilding of San Diego Mission during the deep fall of October 1776. It was necessary to put the 7,000 adobe bricks into place ahead of the approaching rainy season.

On October 25, 1776, with Fray Gregorio Amurrio, eleven soldiers and an equal number of mules bearing packs and provisions, Serra set out for the valley of Capistrano. There he found the cross erected earlier by Lasuén still standing. He had the bells which were buried unearthed and hung from beams, ready to call the heathens to their new Christian home. An *enramada* was set up and an improvised altar placed within it. There, on November 1, 1776, the feast of All Saints, Serra sung a High Mass and declared California's seventh mission founded.

Serra described Capistrano as a "place with abundant water, pasture, firewood and timber," as well as an area containing plentiful Indian *rancherías*. The *Presidente* selected Amurrio and Fray Pablo de Mugartegui as the missionaries for the place, declaring that both were men of "zeal, talent and religious spirit." As a result of their labors, he hoped to see rapid progress made.

On November 3rd, Serra set out for San Gabriel to get a few Christian Indians to serve as interpreters and preceptors of the pagan Indians at Capistrano and to bring provisions and a herd of cattle for the new foundation. While returning to San Juan Capistrano, Serra had a narrow escape. With a single soldier and a San Gabriel Indian, he was ahead of the pack train. Suddenly they came face-to-face with a hostile group of natives, painted and armed, ready to strike. The Gabrieleno Indian yelled out to them in their own tongue, telling them not to kill the *padre* and warning them that there were soldiers close behind. The ruse worked and the Indians desisted.

Serra did not shun the attackers. When they had been pacified, he called to them, traced the sign of the cross over them all, and gave them glass beads. Later, when the *Presidente* related the incident, he said that he thought surely the end had come. After the establishment at San Juan Capistrano was firmly rooted, Serra returned to San Gabriel and then moved on northward to San Luis Obispo with Fray Fermín de Lasuén as his traveling companion.

Passage along the Santa Barbara Channel at that time of year was even more a problem than usual. The winds blew and the rains came down in torrents. The sea was rough and the surf rolled over the sands to the very foot of the mountains. As a result, the friars and their party had to take to the hill trail along the cliffs above it.

Serra related how kind the Indians were to him. Physically weak, he was unable to walk and had to be carried. Of this assistance he wrote: "I could not and cannot repay their charity and their labors as I desire." All of this increased the love he had long had for the *Canaliños*. The *Presidente* probably spent Christmas at San Luis Obispo. He later convinced Lasuén to take on the post of missionary at San Diego. Though at first reluctant, Lasuén eventually "bowed his neck to the yoke."

Early in January, Serra reached his headquarters at San Carlos Borromeo. During his absence, the friars there had baptized twenty-three more persons, bringing the total number of christenings at San Carlos to 441. Also during that time, the *presidio* of San Francisco and Missions San Francisco and Santa Clara had been founded.

There were now eight rungs on the mission ladder.

Two Additional Missions

FRAY Pedro Font's description of the future San Francisco, written on March 28, 1776, is something of a classic:

Indeed, although in my travels I saw very good sites and beautiful country, I saw none which pleased me so much as this. And I think that if it could be well settled like Europe there would not be anything more beautiful in all the world, for it has the best advantages for founding in it a most beautiful city, with all the conveniences desired by land as well as by sea.

Juan Bautista de Anza's exploring party planted a cross on the white steep rock overhanging the Golden Gate where he proposed to establish the *presidio*. From there, the company rode over hills and through valleys and brush in a southeasterly direction, where they came upon two lakes and a delightful creek.

This area they called *Arroyo de los Dolores,* because it was the Feast of Our Lady of Sorrows. Font considered that place "the best for establishing on it one of the two missions" projected for the San Francisco area. The future San Francisco Mission, or Dolores as it came to be known popularly, had indeed a pretty setting. The *padres* chose their sites with very practical ideas in mind, but they never overlooked the element of beauty.

The *presidio* was founded on July 28th. Four days later, work was inaugurated on the mission itself and it is that date which is generally accepted by historians as the official foundation for San Francisco Mission. There is no mention of formal ceremonies: a cross raising, a blessing or other ceremonies, but the founding of a mission did not always follow the same pattern.

Formal ceremonies for the taking possession of the *presidio* occurred on September 17, the Feast of the Stigmata of Saint Francis. The cross was hoisted, blessed and venerated and Fray

Francisco Palou celebrated Holy Mass. Then the officers took formal possession in the name of the king.

All entered the *presidio* chapel singing the *Te Deum*. During the ceremonies, bells were rung, muskets fired and salvos of artillery thundered from the fort. This was the founding of San Francisco. Saint Francis had found and occupied his harbor.

On October 3, Palou had blessed the chapel for the new mission. For that gala occasion, the wooden building was adorned with flags and bunting from the ship *San Carlos*. Six days later, the mission was formally inaugurated. After Mass, a statue of Saint Francis was solemnly carried in procession and placed on the altar. Fire-crackers and rockets added to the festivities. Mission bells pealed forth across the lake.

Palou was now established as a missionary as far north as Spain's power had reached, over a hundred miles further into pagan country than Fray Junípero Serra had yet penetrated. Surely the *Presidente* was there in spirit.

Fernando de Rivera reached San Francisco on November 26th. He carefully inspected the sites of the *presidio* and mission and was pleased with both. He then determined to go ahead with the establishment of Santa Clara in order to fulfill the directives of the viceroy.

An expedition set out for the Rio de Gualadupe, about forty miles southeast, at the northern end of the Santa Clara Valley. They arrived at their destination, a place known as "the Laurel," on January 7th. Five days later Fray Tomas de la Peña raised and blessed the cross at California's eighth mission.

With the founding of Santa Clara, the establishments ordered by the viceroy for the bay area—a *presidio* and two missions—were accomplished facts. A famous son and daughter of the thirteenth century Italian town of Assisi, Francesco and Chiara, now became well known on the Pacific coast of North America.

Authority to Confirm

WITH the arrival of the *Santiago* at Monterey, in June of 1778, Fray Junípero Serra received authorization from Pope Clement XIV to administer the Sacrament of Confirmation to the neophytes of Alta California. It was a privilege the *Presidente* had sought in view of the precedent in Baja California.

Serra also learned that California and the other northern provinces in the viceroyalty of New Spain had been erected into a separate political unit called a commandancy general. Teodoro de Croix had been named to head the new entity.

The new commandant general was to control the military, political, judicial and financial affairs of the jurisdiction. From then onwards, Serra would make his appeals to headquarters in Sonora instead of to Viceroy Bucareli. California and Serra would now be deprived of Bucareli's generosity and sympathy toward the mission enterprise.

This latest division of government complicated the structure of church-state relations. The College of San Fernando remained in Bucareli's jurisdiction and the supply ships provisioning California still sailed out of San Blas, also within the viceroy's command. The new governor, Felipe de Neve, served directly under de Croix who was starting afresh as far as knowledge of the area was concerned, a fact that would necessarily cause delay in rendering decisions.

De Croix was a quick study. He soon came to realize that Fray Junípero Serra had zeal, true religious spirit, prudence in governing the missions and treating with the Indians, as well as solicitude for the general welfare.

At Carmel and Monterey, Serra announced receipt of the faculty to confirm and set a date for the ceremonies—the feast of Sts. Peter and Paul, June 29th. The adults were to be instructed as to the nature of the sacrament and sponsors were to be sought among the soldiers, servants, workmen and Baja California Indians living in the area.

On the morning of June 29th, Serra sung a High Mass, had the *doctrina* recited and preached on the nature of the sacrament. He carefully explained how he, a simple priest, had been specially empowered to confirm in the absence of a bishop. Then the *Presidente* proceeded to administer the first confirmations within the limits of the present State of California.

After the ceremonies, he started a new book of records, his *Libro de Confirmaciones,* in which he inserted a copy of the decree authorizing him to confirm. Then, in his own hand, Serra entered the facts of each individual, giving the name, age, place of origin and name of sponsor.

Meanwhile, the governor added a "little grain of pepper . . . as a condiment" to the occasion by questioning whether the missions were canonically subject to the bishop of Durango or Guadalajara. The suggestion would later blossom into a full blown controversy.

On August 24th, the seventh anniversary of the planting of the cross in the Carmel Valley, Serra set out by sea for San Diego. It was a long voyage which ended only in mid September. Though the *Presidente* went south primarily to administer the Sacrament of Confirmation, he was also there to console and aid the missionaries in their many problems. Theirs were uphill labors, trying to rebuild the Christianity that had almost been wiped out and attempting to make the economically poor mission prosper.

The Visitation Northwards

U PON returning to San Diego, Fray Junípero Serra found that the area was still a dangerous frontier mission. But he did have the privilege of confirming three of the former pagan Indians who had killed Fray Luis Jayme. The *Presidente* confirmed at San Diego on twelve days until October 18th. Most of those were Indians, a few Spaniards, among the latter the sons of the *presidio* commander, Jose Francisco Ortega. Altogether six hundred and ten confirmations were administered.

At San Juan Capistrano, Serra confirmed 163 persons. He was delighted with the progress made in two years at this "new planting," and he praised the work of the Indian interpreters. He found one hundred and twenty-five Christians actually living at the mission.

Then on to San Gabriel, where a goodly number of Indians were awaiting to receive the sacrament. Hastily, the *Presidente* completed his work and then journeyed on through the San Fernando Valley, the hill country of present-day Ventura county, across the Santa Clara Valley and its river to the place of Asumpta, where he ardently desired a mission.

The arduous passage along the beach and cliffs of the Channel came next, through modern Santa Barbara, past Gaviota and Point Conception. Serra recorded no incidents along the way. He must have ridden for he made the long journey in seven days. At San Luis Obispo and San Antonio, the *Presidente* again confirmed. By the time his journey was completed, Fray Junípero Serra had administered the sacrament to no fewer than 1,897.

By the time Serra arrived back at San Carlos, to celebrate Christmas, he was "completely worn out." But he noted that "during my extensive journey, I encountered no mishap or adverse effects." It was successful in every way, especially spiritually.

There were many problems of an economical nature facing the friars. Feeding and clothing the Indians was difficult in the early days. The catechumens and the baptized Christians, according to the mission system, were to live in the missions. Therefore the friars had to proceed cautiously, so they would not accept more converts at any one mission than they could provide for. Hence, in the early years, baptism was often deferred unless there was danger of death.

The number of baptisms often depended on the bushels of beans, corn and wheat available to feed them. And, to further complicate matters, the governor could determine whether or not double rations were to be allowed. The "double ration" helped to a great extent to bridge the scarcity of food. For example, Fray Fermín Lasuén at San Diego stated in 1777 that by means of the double rations, he was able to maintain five Baja California Indians, shepherds, interpreters, the sick, some orphans and a few laborers.

Ultimately, all rations were suspended to the missions and somehow the foundations managed to survive, though with some difficulty. Perhaps it was a blessing in disguise, because it forced the friars to work even harder in their attempts to make each establishment self-supporting.

Problems, problems everywhere could have been Serra's lament. Yet the tone of his letters indicates that stubborn resiliency built into the fabric of truly great people. Once, when complaining about the governor's unreasonableness, the *Presidente* noted that "this gentleman has the special grace of divesting me of any self-love I might still possess."

Confirmation Controversy

THE so-called "Confirmation controversy" was long a source of agitation to Fray Junípero Serra and the other missionaries in Alta California. Worse than that, it infringed on the spiritual welfare of the neophytes because it threatened to deprive them of the sacrament.

By virtue of the *Patronato Real*, papal briefs issued in favor of New Spain required the royal *pase* before they could be implemented. In addition, the viceroy or his delegate also enjoyed the privilege of issuing the *pase* in his designated territory. Governor Felipe de Neve was not unwilling to affix his *pase* to the document from Pope Clement XIV authorizing him to confirm, but Serra did not have in hand the document. It was at the Franciscan headquarters in Mexico City.

The *Presidente* and the governor held several lengthy conferences about the issue, but the governor insisted that he had to comply with the directives of issuing the *pase* only on presentation of the official documents. Throughout this entire case, neither Serra nor the officials at San Fernando College ever brought up the question as to whether a papal document treating purely spiritual things actually depended on the royal *pase* for its use and execution. Had such an argument been used, the missionary work might have been greatly hampered.

The friars had to fit their activity into the strong regalism of the eighteenth century if they wished to accomplish anything at all. They were consistently careful that all the negotiations were conducted in a friendly manner. It was a battle of wits over the interpretation of the *Patronato*.

Serra's conscience was clear. He confirmed by the delegated authority of the pope. Hence the confirmations he conferred were valid and licit. As far as the royal patronage was concerned, Serra at no time denied that it applied, but he maintained that its demands had been met.

The *Presidente* also used the practical argument that spiritual damage and scandal would result if he ceased to confirm. It was a delicate situation. Had he been hot-headed and loose of tongue, he might have stirred up trouble among the people. He was careful to be prudent, lest the disagreement leak out to them.

Neve represented the strongly regalistic position of the king. As vice-patron of the king over the province of California, he had been vigilant from the start concerning the royal *pase*. At first, like Serra, he presumed the *pase* had been given and even told Serra he could confirm.

However, when he received the royal *cedula* of November 23, 1777, tightening up the operational directives of the *Patronato Real* the governor felt obliged to direct Serra to stop confirming until the actual papers arrived. It was a matter of interpretation. Neve interpreted the matter strictly, Serra did so liberally.

Writing later about the matter, Fray Francisco Palou imputed no evil intentions to Neve. He said "we are not to believe that the governor did this through malice, but as he had no advisor near, he acted according to his best judgement, presuming that this was what he ought to do." Nor did Serra calumniate Neve. He merely called him sagacious, a quality which the *Presidente* on another occasion said he would have to match with the wisdom of the serpent.

It was obvious enough that the vexing question, and it was a terribly important one to the friars, could not be settled on Monterey. For a while, at least, the conferral of confirmation would have to be halted.

Voice for American Independence

THE effect on far-away California of the move for American Independence has yet to be adequately documented, for communications were practically nonexistent. As a province, the destinies of California were totally interlinked with those of its Spanish mother country.

By virtue of the so-called Family Compact between the Bourbon crowns, Spain joined France, on June 23, 1779, in the war against England on behalf of the American colonies. It was a calculated risk. Victory would mean autonomy for England's New World possessions, thus resulting in the appearance of a dangerous neighbor, in America, and the eventual loss, perhaps, of Spain's colonial empire.

Fray Junípero Serra learned about the hostilities while visiting San Francisco. He was asked to offer public prayers for the favorable outcome of the Spanish maneuvers and to collect one *peso* from every Indian in support of the war effort.

In deference to the wishes of Madrid officials, Serra informed his fellow missionaries, on June 15, 1780, that "because we are in a special manner indebted here to the piety of our Catholic Monarch, who provides for us as his minister chaplains, and poor Franciscans . . . and because we are interested in the success and victory of his Catholic armed forces . . . I most earnestly ask in the Lord that as soon as you receive this letter you be most attentive in begging God to grant success to this public cause which is so favorable to our holy Catholic and Roman Church and is most pleasing in the sight of the same God Our Lord."

Noting that "our Catholic Sovereign is at war with perfidious heretics," [i.e., the English], Father Serra felt that "we should all be united in this purpose and display how we are one in spirit, an especial reason for offering to God Our Lord our most pleasing if poor prayers." The missionaries were directed to recite, at the principal Mass on Sundays, the litany of the Blessed Mother or the saints along with the psalm, verses and prayers prescribed by the *Rituale Romanum* for "time of war."

At the conclusion of the services, all were instructed to say the *Credo* three times "to help to soften the pride of our enemies who surround us on all sides and who, from time to time, threaten us."

To what extent the struggle for American independence actually affected the California scene is unknown. The Pacific area was not attacked for England had enough to do on the Atlantic coast with her rebellious colonies.

One of the few references to the cause was recorded by Benjamin Cummings Truman in 1867, while on a visit to Mission San Juan Capistrano. There Father Joseph Mut reportedly showed him "an old record kept by *Padre* Gorgonio [Gregorio Amurrio]" which bore the words:

We prayed fervently last evening for the success of the colonists under one George Washington, because we believe their cause is just and that the Great Redeemer is on their side.

That comment dated May 7, 1778, is now a valuable piece of "fugitive" Californiana.

Presidente *on the Move*

THE long and complicated controversy about Fray Junípero Serra's authorization to confirm was finally settled in December of 1780. The viceroy was advised by his counsel that "Serra was not to be impeded from administering the sacrament in the towns of the missions entrusted to the Observant Fathers of their Apostolic College." Morever the viceroy was told that Serra "is to be given those aids necessary to that end which he might request and need, and as a result of this measure," the *Presidente* was to be notified immediately.

It had been a struggle of wills. The Caesaro-papistic administration of the Catholic monarch whom Serra often described as "the most pious in the whole world" had interfered with the sacramental work of the *Presidente* for over a year. But now confirmations could again proceed.

On October 7, 1781, Carmel experienced a slight earthquake. Serra reported that the only damage sustained was the breaking of a flask of brandy at Santa Clara which "the poor Fathers were saving for an emergency." Several weeks later, the *Presidente* was called upon to perform a duty he had never met before, that of bringing spiritual comfort to a man destined for execution. Juan Antonio Labra, a *presidio* soldier, had been condemned to death by the governor because "he broke the seventh commandment." He must have stolen a goodly amount to merit the death sentence, Neve ordered him to be hung, but since no hangman was available, the sentence was commuted to shooting.

Serra resumed his confirmation tours. Upon arriving at Santa Clara, he laid the cornerstone of the new adobe church. The original site of the mission had proven too low and suffered heavy inundations. Hence the new edifice was being built at a new site, about a mile and a half south of the original foundation.

After the ceremony, Serra and Fray Juan Crespi immediately set out for Carmel. After only a short jaunt, Serra's mule shied and threw him into a field. As the *Presidente* described it, "the mule which was carrying this cargo threw him with a lively thrust." His companions rode into nearby San Jose to get the doctor.

Serra was in considerable pain, especially in one of his hands and in the ribs. When the doctor arrived, he assured the friar that all his bones were in place. The following day, Serra continued his journey, though with difficulty. He mended well, and shortly thereafter could write that "little by little, I was relieved of the pain and now all is past. Blessed be God!"

Serra's student and long-time companion, Fray Juan Crespi, became ill after the return to Carmel. None of the usual remedies worked and the sixty-year old Indian missionary passed away on January 1, 1782.

Next day, after a requiem High Mass, Crespi's remains in a redwood coffin were lowered by Serra into a grave in the sanctuary near the main altar. The Mallorcan born friar had followed Serra into the Sierra Gorda, then to Baja California and finally to Alta California. His missionary career was not particularly colorful, but it was solid and continuous. His early explorations will always be his chief title to fame. Herbert Eugene Bolton said that in Crespi's diaries "the human toils, the adventures, the thrills, the hopes, the fears of three historic journeys on the Pacific Coast are embalmed."

So the first of the Mallorcan triumvirate of Serra, Palou and Crespi was now gone. His remains still rest at San Carlos Mission in Carmel, alongside those of his devoted teacher and mentor.

Serra and the Bishopric

IT has long been the practice of the Holy See to bestow broad faculties on certain priests laboring in missionary areas regarding the administration of the sacraments. One such prerogative, generally delegated to local superiors, concerns the conferral of Confirmation, a faculty customarily reserved, in most parts of the Christian world, for those enjoying episcopal ordination.

Such an apostolic concession was exercised in California by Fray Junípero Serra. The venerable Franciscan *Presidente* sought and received authorization "so that he could visit the missions and confirm the neophytes, lest they be deprived of the great spiritual good to be had from the effects of this holy sacrament."

Judging from remarks of his biographer, there were those apparently who viewed such actions on Serra's part as indicative of episcopal aspirations. Not so, according to Francisco Palou: Junípero Serra "was so far removed from seeking this dignity or even desiring it, that he rather devised means to flee it, because of his profound humility and his fervent desire to labor in the vineyard of the Lord."

Palou further mentioned that after the establishment of Mission San Carlos, "His Reverence learned that a courier at Madrid had written to the Reverend Father Guardian of our college . . . that a great honor was waiting the Reverend Father Junípero." When word reached Monterey of the "great honor," Serra, "fearful that he would lose before God the merit of his labors in these spiritual Conquests through receiving in this world the reward that was foretold in that letter," immediately resolved to refuse the distinction or any other which would forestall his being able to live "as an apostolic missionary among the infidels and to shed his blood for their conversion."

Palou confided that Serra may not have made a vow to that effect, "though I am inclined to believe he did, for he did not explain the matter to me in full detail."

The possibility of such an appointment was not so remote as might initially appear. A diocese was established at Sonora in 1779, for example, while that vast area was almost entirely missionary territory. One outstanding Franciscan historian states categorically that "Spain should have asked for a bishop for the Californias, considering the huge territory, even though churches were few and the income nothing."

So disturbed was the *Presidente* at the thought of becoming a bishop that he took the extreme precaution of writing an influential acquaintance at the royal court asking him to serve "rather as his censor than as his agent," if the issue of bestowing regal favors on his person ever came up for discussion.

At a meeting of the Newman Club, held at Los Angeles on May 26, 1910, John Steven McGroarty had this to say about the Franciscan *Presidente* and the bishopric:

I always think of Father Junípero Serra as the first bishop of the Diocese of Monterey-Los Angeles. He was never consecrated as a bishop, but he exercised some of the faculties of the high and holy office. For a time he was empowered to administer the Sacrament of Confirmation, and many thousands of Indians, together with a large number of white persons were confirmed by him.

In addition to this, he was the first President of the California Missions, in which capacity he directed the work of the Church here and exercised authority over priests and people. Father Junípero was, therefore, in effect a bishop, although not one in fact.

Foundation of Los Angeles

THE Franciscans who made their way along *El Camino Real* during the seventy-nine years after 1769, measured up remarkably well to the ideals outlined at the General Chapter of the Order, convened at Interama in 1500. There it was agreed that only "the best and the most pious friars, who, being of tried virtue and learning, can give a good example to the pagans and Christians with whom they may come in contact, should be the ones sent to the missions."

Statistically, 142 friars from New Spain's three Apostolic Colleges of San Fernando (Mexico City), Nuestra Señora de Guadalupe (Zacatecas) and Santa Cruz (Querétaro) invested 2,269 man years along the Pacific Slope to bring into the Christian fold and into the Hispanic civilization nearly one hundred thousand aborigines, while they also attended to the spiritual needs of the conquering Spaniards and Mexicans in *presidios, pueblos* and *ranchos.*

Their period of service in "this last corner of the earth" ranged from the few months of Fray Julian Lopez to the forty-four years of Fray Jose Ramon Abella. The story of those heroic evangelizers who, two centuries ago, effected the first triumph of religion and civilization in what is now the State of California, is typified by their imprint on the earliest annals of Los Angeles.

Ironically, though the *pueblo* was named for *Nuestra Señora de los Angeles,* the Franciscans were initially opposed in principle to its actual founding. Fray Junípero Serra felt that the establishment of Spanish towns was still premature, fearing "that they would be prejudicial to Indian and mission rights." History proved him right.

Despite the *Presidente's* openly-expressed view that the government should have waited until the missionary outposts were further developed, authorities at Madrid decided that *pueblos* at San Jose and Los Angeles were vital to the overall objective of obtaining a small indigenous population, Spanish in its sympathy, and partly Spanish in blood, to produce soldiers for the missions and *presidios* at the sea-ports, and to plant the germ of a future Spanish-American province.

The *Pueblo de Nuestra Señora de los Angeles* was established on September 4, 1781, within the parochial confines of San Gabriel Mission, with a contingency of eleven families, or forty-four people. Four square leagues of land, good for planting all kinds of grains and seeds, about three-fourths of a mile west of the river, on a ledge rising above the present Alameda Street, were set aside for the further extention in the presidial district of San Diego de Alcalá.

Fray Junípero Serra first visited the Pueblo de *Nuestra Señora de los Angeles* on March 18, 1782, seven months after its foundation. He referred to the town endearingly as *La Portiuncula,* but he did not describe it.

Though Serra and his confreres harbored serious reservations about the expediency of establishing the *pueblo,* the foundation, like its sister metropolis to the north, bears that distinctively Seraphic imprint that can only be predicated of the earliest penetrators into the far-away Province of California.

Franciscan influence in Los Angeles reflects, at the local level, what the friars accomplished along the whole expanse of the Pacific Slope. Even Governor Pedro Fages admitted, in 1789, "that the rapid, pleasing and interesting progress both in spiritual and temporal matters . . . are the glorious effect of the apostolic zeal, activity and indefatigable labors of these missionaries."

Care for the Canaliños

FROM the earliest years of the conquest, Spanish explorers and colonists noted that the Indians of the Santa Barbara Channel were distinct from the other aborigines between San Diego and San Francisco. Those peoples formed a separate linguistic group and were more advanced in the arts and crafts than any other coastal tribe that came under Hispanic influence.

They were of particular interest to Fray Junípero Serra and received much attention on the part of both Church and state. Five missions were eventually established among them. Of these Serra founded the first two.

In late March of 1782, Jose Ortega led a contingency of soldiers and their families, some Christian Indians, muleteers, cattle and pack animals bearing utensils for house and field and church ornaments north from San Gabriel to finally establish the long-contemplated mission dedicated to San Buenaventura. Ortega led the cavalcade across the hills of Ventura County and the fertile valley of Santa Clara to where the bare hills came down to meet the sea. Ahead lay Asumpta, an Indian town of five hundred inhabitants where the mission was to be located.

On Easter Sunday morning, Fray Junípero Serra blessed the site, under the shadow of the hills not far from the river and close to the sea. The cross was raised and blessed. The *Presidente* offered Holy Mass and preached. Afterwards the soldiers took possession of the land in the name of the king, permission having been obtained from the natives through interpreters to settle there. Then followed the chanting of the *Te Deum*. Serra had founded his ninth and last mission in Alta California.

The day was one of special joy. The neighboring Indians were friendly and demonstrated their pleasure. There were many Christians present with all the soldiers and their families. For the celebration a young bull was killed and the meat distributed among the people. For the friars and the military officers a sheep was slain—for it had been the custom in Mallorca to eat lamb on Easter.

Later, speaking about the event, Serra said: "I cannot make this letter too long by describing the joyful demonstrations of the pagans of the vicinity and the excellence of the site." Serra inscribed the title pages of the registers and then later wrote to Fray Fermín Lasuén: "I have desired for many years to see the mission of Our Seraphic Doctor, San Buenaventura, established. Concerning this foundation, we can say what was said when the saint was canonized: 'The longer it took, the more solemnly did we celebrate.' "

The *Presidente* now had nine missions. Concerning the latest one he wrote to his guardian: "This much I will say that the college can now rely on having a mission which will be second to none among those founded, and in a short time it will surpass the others."

This was indeed high praise for San Buenaventura, considering the vast extent and fertility of San Gabriel. The only misgiving Serra had was the difficulty of bringing water from the river to the future grain fields. And even that problem had a solution. Before Serra left San Buenaventura, Fray Pedro Benito Cambon had demonstrated how the water could be channeled to where it was needed.

It was a noble beginning and one long overdue. San Buenaventura Mission would thrive and eventually become the southland's first canonical parish, thus escaping the ruin and abandonment experienced by so many of the other establishments along *El Camino Real*.

Presidio
at Santa Barbara

ON April 15, 1782, Fray Junípero Serra set out with the pack train from San Buenaventura. Following the shoreline closely for about twenty-five miles, they reached the present city of Santa Barbara the same day. For some reason the *Presidente* did not like the site chosen and said that it was not a good place for either a *presidio* or a mission. It was one of Serra's few mistakes for the area developed more than he envisioned. In majestic setting and in the splendor of its architecture, it is without a rival among the California missions today.

But Serra was considering the situation as he saw it then. With so many natives in the area, a large water supply was needed and extensive tracts of land for farm and pasturage. The area around Santa Barbara simply did not appear to be adequate.

Very likely Serra had in mind the Goleta area, near the present-day airport and the University of California. Both Crespi and Font had indicated that as a favorable mission site. Or possibly he was thinking of the Carpinteria Valley. Later Montecito was spoken of as the area which afforded the best opportunity for a successful mission.

In any event, on Sunday morning, April 21st, ground was blessed, the cross raised and blessed, and Fray Junípero Serra sang a High Mass. Afterwards he preached and then all joined in the *Alabado*. Serra inscribed a set of register books, calling the new foundation "this new Mission and Royal *Presidio* of Santa Barbara." There was no doubt in his mind that he had founded a mission.

The *Presidente* expected that the *presidio*-mission would be a temporary combination and he waited at Santa Barbara for several weeks for Governor Felipe de Neve to indicate when the separate mission would be founded. Little did he know then that it would be another four years before the establishment would be made.

There are few detailed documents on the early developments at the Santa Barbara *presidio*. There were many Indians in the region and they were friendly and cooperative. Neve noted in a letter that the "numerous Indians who inhabit the Channel remain quiet and tranquil . . . and they have gladly and voluntarily labored on the buildings of the *presidio* and the aqueduct."

The *presidio* was located in what was for many years the geographical center of the later city of Santa Barbara—centered about the juncture of Cañon Perdido and Santa Barbara streets. The adobe church which was subsequently built faced the south. It was used as the *presidio* and town church until 1854, when it was torn down.

Neve was rattling the cage of the friars. He vigorously complained about their manner of founding and maintaining the missions, all the while threatening to devise a better formula for them to follow. It must have been a momentary aberration because two years later this same man, then commandant general of the *Provincias Internas,* said that the Franciscans in Alta California operated the best institutions of any in the entire province.

When Neve told Serra that the mission at Santa Barbara would not be built until the *presidio* was finished, the *Presidente* decided to return to San Carlos Borromeo. He left for the north on May 6th. He arrived at Carmel on the vigil of Pentecost, his leg in a swollen condition. Happily, by mid July he was well again and able to resume his hectic schedule of activities. But the tone of his letters indicated that he knew his days were fast coming to a close.

Last Confirmation Tour

THOUGH suffering from severe pains in his chest, Fray Junípero Serra was determined to make a final tour of all the missions before his faculty to confirm expired on July 10, 1784. He decided to take advantage of an available ship to begin the long journey. Serra was conscious of the bad state of his health, but the possibility of imminent death did not occur to him. His determination to achieve his purpose was as strong as in 1750 and 1769.

First he sailed to Santa Barbara, then on to San Buenaventura. On September 6th, he arrived at San Diego and then moved on to San Juan Capistrano. At San Gabriel, Serra's health was very poor. The friars there worried that he was about to die. Yet Serra continued his prayers, offered Holy Mass and confirmed. He even found time to write some important letters.

Back north he went, visiting San Buenaventura again and the *presidio* at Santa Barbara. Then on to San Luis Obispo. At San Antonio he confirmed 292 persons. He arrived back at San Carlos on December 15th. In April, the *Presidente* left for Santa Clara to dedicate a new church. After the ceremony, he spent some days in spiritual exercises, preparing for death. It was a precious time for Serra and Fray Francisco Palou.

Back at Carmel, the *Presidente* continued to work at his usual place. Serra continued to baptize occasionally. His last conferral of that sacrament was on August 2nd. Of the 1,014 persons baptized at San Carlos since its foundation, Serra had personally participated at 540. He had assisted at 182 of the 258 marriages and recorded 151 of the 377 deaths since 1770.

Serra never stated that he ever walked between any of the missions during his years in Alta California, except perhaps for some distance along the Santa Barbara coast in 1777. Fray Francisco Palou on only one occasion declared that Serra walked. He always had to travel with a military escort and, of necessity had to keep up with his escort. His biographer concluded that the *Presidente* walked only once from one mission to another.

Considering the difficulties of travelling, Serra's journeys were remarkable. Between the years 1769 and 1784, when he was between the ages of fifty-six and seventy, he made the following voyages by sea: from San Diego to Monterey in 1770; from San Diego to San Blas in 1772; From San Blas to San Diego in 1774; from Monterey to San Diego in 1776, 1778 and 1783.

By land the *Presidente* travelled the entire distance between San Diego and Monterey five times; between Monterey and San Francisco eight times; between Monterey and San Juan Capistrano seven times; between Monterey and San Antonio eleven times. He also made a round trip between Monterey and Soledad once and another round trip from Carmel deep into the Santa Lucia Mountains into the Esselen territory.

Then there were innumerable trips between Monterey and Carmel. To these must be added the round trip between San Blas and Mexico City in 1772 and 1773. Serra's sea mileage for his California career amounted to approximately 5,400 miles; his land mileage about 5,525 miles. This was quite an accomplishment for an old infirm man under the physical and social travel conditions of his day.

Towards the Ramparts of Eternity

W HEN Fray Junípero Serra founded San Carlos Mission, in 1770, he inscribed the register for deaths and burials with these words: *"Omnes morimur et quasi aqua dilabimur in terram, qua non revertuntur."* ("We all die, and like waters that return no more, we fall down into the earth.") It was no time for Serra to live out that axiom.

In quiet pursuits and in more dangerous moments, Serra had kept the purpose of life, based on Christian faith. He had faced death many times. He once told the viceroy that he lived as close to the arrows as any soldier. Death held no terror for the *Presidente*.

Now he was seventy years old. He had taken his last earthly journey to bestow a spiritual benefit and for the last time he looked upon the California he had helped to bring into being.

When Fray Francisco Palou arrived at San Carlos, on August 18, 1784, he found Serra in a weakened condition, suffering from heaviness in his chest and the usual swelling of the legs. However, he was up and around. That morning he had sung High Mass and preached. In the afternoon, he went to the mission church and recited with the neophytes the *doctrina*.

Later, when the *Presidente* asked for Holy Viaticum, he insisted on walking to the Church. With a white stole over his gray habit, Serra walked unaided and went directly to the sanctuary where he knelt on a *priedieu*. For some time afterwards, he knelt in prayer. Then, in the company with the soldiers and Indians, he returned to his cell.

A few hours later, Palou visited Serra in his cell. There he came upon the *presidio* carpenter. Asked his business, the man told Palou that Serra had called for him to prepare his coffin. The *Presidente* spent the rest of the day in silence, seated on his chair and taking only a little broth as nourishment. That night he was anointed.

Serra passed the greater part of his last night on earth on his knees, pressing his pained chest against the rough boards of his bed. At dawn, he appeared to be relieved of pain and suffering less congestion of the chest. He was seated on his rush stool, leaning against his bed. On the pillow lay the foot long crucifix which he had carried with him in his apostolic wanderings since 1750.

The founder of the California missions fell asleep in the Lord in the early afternoon of August 28th. Palou closed the eyes of his superior and friend and said his *"Requiescat in pace!"* Junípero Serra had died in the midst of his labors. He had lived seventy years nine months and four days. Peace and rest were finally his. Though the man who had coveted a martyr's crown had died quietly, the closing scenes of his life were peculiarly dramatic.

Palou told the Indians to toll the church bells to announce the *Presidente's* demise. They sounded the *doble,* the signal of death even today in Mallorca. The entire Christian village assembled.

Serra's Franciscan habit now became his shroud. The remains were placed in the coffin and alongside it were placed six lighted candles. The door of the cell was then opened and, until nightfall, Indians and Spaniards entered the room and prayed for the *"Santo Padre."*

Presidente *Laid to Rest*

THE solemn funeral of Fray Junípero Serra took place at San Carlos on Sunday morning, August 29, 1784. Representatives of all the elements of the friar's diversified life participated at the ceremonies.

Among the mourners were the six hundred Indian converts living at the mission, the mission guard, the men from the *presidio*, the officers and most of the crew of the *San Carlos*. Europe, North and South America; Mallorca, Mexico, Baja California and the Sierra Gorda; the army and the navy, the professions and the artisans and the toilers; all were represented.

There were Indians who had come from practically every *ranchería* in the area of Carmel. During the fourteen years of established mission life at San Carlos, Serra and his co-workers had extended their evangelizing efforts nearly thirty miles south, twenty miles north and twenty miles east of the actual mission. One of the mourners was Bernardino de Jesus Fages, the very first one Serra had baptized in California, on December 26, 1770, and now one of the *fiscales* of the mission.

Throughout the day, at half hour intervals, a cannon shot was fired from the *San Carlos* and answered by a volley from the cannons of the *presidio*. The reverberations were heard in the Carmel Valley. The *doble* of the mission bells and the firing of the cannons "melted the hearts of all," according to Fray Francisco Palou.

Within the crowded church, a vigil was solemnly kept, followed by a solemn requiem Mass. It was celebrated by Palou. The Indian choir provided the music and army and naval officers held lighted candles. Interestingly, there is no mention of a homily. Serra's life was its own homily, perhaps that was recognized even then.

Burial was deferred until afternoon. In the meantime some of the people remained in the church, viewing the remains, praying and touching them with their medals and rosaries. At four o'clock, the bells called all the people together again. A procession was formed. The officers alternated bearing on their shoulders the remains of the *Presidente*.

The procession was held in the courtyard or patio of the mission enclosure. Four stops were made during its course, during which a response was sung. The procession then re-entered the church and the bearers placed the coffin on a table at the foot of the altar.

The open grave was blessed and incensed. The last prayers were said and the mortal remains of Fray Junípero Serra were lowered into the opening in the sanctuary floor, close to those of Fray Juan Crespi. Another response was sung, "the tears, sighs and cries of those assisting drowning out the voices of the chanters." Then the congregation dispersed. Seventy laborious years were a part of history.

When Palou gave one of Serra's handkerchiefs to Dr. Juan Garcia, the royal physician, the doctor said "with this little cloth, I expect to effect more cures than with all my books and pharmacy."

Serra's Sarcophagus at Carmel

THE sarcophagus of Fray Junípero Serra, at Mission San Carlos Borromeo, is a synthesis of the early Catholic history in the far-away province of California. Designed by the noted Catalan sculptor, Joseph A. Mora, "it depicts Father Serra lying in state, with his close associates, Fathers Crespi, Lopez and Lasuén, Serra's successor as President of the Missions, grouped around the main body of the sarcophagus."

The *dramatis personae* of the Alta California conquest are represented as Spanish soldiers, Franciscans, Indians in their wild and native state, and the neophytes as they are Christianized. They appear in panels on the side.

At the side of the handsome art-form, is a medallion of Carlos, King of Spain, and of the Pope who gave the friars their authority in matters of local development. Seven low flat bas-reliefs in bronze picture the historical events in California, such as the first Mass, the first baptism and the miracle of the ship, San Antonio, in San Diego Bay. Also portrayed is the Indian uprising at the first of the Franciscan missionary foundations. The Spanish coat-of-arms, with the Franciscan cord denoting the order, is shown interwoven with a garland of California poppies at the foot.

The whole creation is executed in bronze and California travatine marble, and is original as well as beautiful in its thought and execution. Critics agree that it is among the finest of Mora's artistic masterpieces.

It is entirely appropriate that the monument should be erected in Carmel, for to Serra that was the most beloved of all the missions. His home was there, and there he died. His body now rests under the pavement on the Gospel side of the mission church.

An account of the Mora sarcophagus, published in the *Catholic News* of New York, on July 29, 1922, states that "now, nearly two hundred years later, it is 'Hail, Junípero Serra!' He has exemplified the mystic paradox of the grain of mustard seed of his Master's parable, that was cast into the earth, and died, so that from it might spring a mighty tree.

"He humbled himself—and now he is exalted. He made himself least—and now he is among the foremost. At his birthplace the King of Spain lately unveiled a monument and dedicated a plaza to Mallorca's great son. The mighty commonwealth of the New World, the cornerstone of whose civilization he helped to lay in the western wilderness, a few years ago officially celebrated his two-hundredth anniversary.

"The most successful drama ever written and produced in the West spreads his name and glory through the effective suggestion of theatrical appeal among the people of the land. To his lonely grave, in the Mission San Carlos de Carmelo, which for generations remained unknown, yearly go thousands of pilgrims in homage to his memory. And there this fall will be dedicated "the memorial which will perpetuate the fame and honor which now belong to Father Junípero Serra, to whom fame and honor meant nothing.

"Yet, it is well that fame and honor should be his just because he did not seek these things but sought only the Kingdom of God."

Legend of Greatness

T HOUGH unknown to Fray Junípero Serra, several years
prior to his death, Felipe de Neve declared that the California
missions were the best in the entire *Provincias Internas*, despite
the fact that they were the most recently established. Certainly
that statement was an oblique tribute to the dynamic and zealous
man who founded them.

A few years after the *Presidente's* demise, Pedro Fages stated that
in all fairness he was forced to say that the condition of the missions
was due to the indefatigable labors of the missionaries in California
"from the beginning." Serra was there "from the beginning" and
he was their founder. To have heard such an encomium from
Fages would surely have pleased Serra.

Fages had earlier maintained that Serra was opposed to all the
measures of the government. He was not asked his opinions or
consulted, but merely given orders. He spoke out whenever he
thought it needful. And his disagreement was resented. Both Neve
and Fages expected Serra to be a loyal vassal, a workhorse, to obey
and not to meddle in the high affairs of government. Those were
the days before "loyal opposition" was tolerated.

Yet Neve and Fages, two opponents of Serra, unequivocally
stated that the work given to him was executed most successfully.
Much less would have been done had not Serra struggled to
accomplish as much as he could.

In his diary of 1769, Costanso states that neither Serra's
advanced years nor the extreme hardships of journeys could
restrain the ardent zeal that animated him for the conversion of
the natives. Galvez praised Serra's great faith and desired in no
way to interfere with its expression.

Fray Rafael Verger, later a bishop, extolled Serra's humility,
his great patience, his uncomplaining spirit through twenty years.
He stressed the man's learning. Fray Perez de Mezquia called
Serra a good missionary, an exemplary religious and an industrious

man. Pablo Font described Serra as a "holy man," a "true apostle," one who was humble, charitable and mortified. These words were not a eulogy, but were written during Serra's life.

Viceroy Antonio Bucareli frequently praised Serra for his zeal, fervor, industry and "forgiving spirit." Fray Fermín Francisco de Lasuén, despite his differences with Serra, thought of him as a "holy man" and a most exemplary superior. He stated that "wherever (Serra) was and wherever he went he was considered a man of exemplary virtue."

Fray Juan Sancho who knew Serra in Mallorca and in Baja California and who became his superior, tells us that Serra was considered "a holy man and his actions those of an apostle." He added that such was the general opinion of those who knew Serra since he had arrived in the New World in 1750.

Fray Juan Gregorio Campos stated that he "had the good fortune of knowing and dealing with the Venerable Father and certainly in his appearance and comportment one could note the most exact observance of the Seraphic Rule, the most continuous mortification of his soul, the most humble wisdom, the ardent zeal for the conversion of pagans and the moral reformation of Christians." Fray Pablo Mugartegui who accompanied Serra to California in 1774 and who later labored under him in California for ten years, declared that Serra was "beloved of God and man."

After Serra died, people, considering him a saint, prayed to him for favors. Hundreds are doing that today. One could hardly call this a conspiracy. The testimony of holiness cannot be contained.

Sanctity and Practicality

SANCTITY is obviously a necessary requirement before anyone can ever be proposed for sainthood. In the case of Fray Junípero Serra, one is impressed by the almost universal testimony of those who knew and worked alongside the friar.

The notion of Serra's sanctity is not a modern one. Shortly after his death, for example, his superior at San Fernando College, in Mexico City, wrote to the Franciscan provincial of Mallorca:

> We have just received the sad news of the death of our beloved countryman, Fr. Junípero Serra. He died a saint's death, and under such extraordinary circumstances, that all those present were highly edified. They all hold the firm conviction that his soul went joyfully to meet its account, and that it was carried across Purgatory without any scorching of its flames, straight to heaven.

He went on to observe that "all say he was a saint, and that his actions have always been those of an apostle. This is the opinion held by all, since he arrived in this kingdom of New Spain, and has continued without interruption and grown stronger up to his much lamented, irreparable death."

After hearing of Serra's demise, Fray Pablo Mugartegui wrote from San Juan Capistrano that "in these past four months we have baptized more pagans than in the past three years. We attribute these conversions to the intercession of our Venerable Father Junípero, who is asking this from God, just as he ceaselessly asked it during life; and we piously believe that he is enjoying God, and that with greater fervor he will ask that favor from the Lord."

Serra's fame for sanctity endured too. On October 2, 1851, Father Jose Villarasa, one of California's pioneer Dominicans, wrote to Barcelona, noting that "I am the chaplain for the convent in Monterey, and for the church of Carmel." The latter "was founded by Fr. Junípero Serra, a Franciscan of Mallorca, who died in the odor of sanctity."

Finally, just a century ago, Serra's death was commemorated at Carmel. Archbishop Joseph Sadoc Alemany and Bishop Eugene O'Connell attended. Father Joachim Adam, Vicar General for the Diocese of Monterey-Los Angeles concluded the homily with the hope that Serra would soon be canonized and placed on the Church's calendar as St. Junípero.

Charles Chapman, an outstanding California historian of an earlier era, said that Serra's "legendary fame attracted Californians to the story of the past. . . . The real Serra was indeed a remarkable man. Already at an advanced age when he came to Alta California, he nevertheless possessed the traits which were most needed in the pioneer.

"He was an enthusiastic, battling, almost quarrelsome, fearless, keenwitted, fervidly devout, unselfish, single-minded missionary. He subordinated everything, and himself most of all, to the demands of his evangelical task." Withal, his administration as Father President was so sound and his grasp of the needs of the province so clear that he was able to exercise a greater authority than ordinarily would have been permitted.

"Though he fought with local governors, he won the confidence of Bucareli, who preferred his judgment to that of Fages or Rivera. Thus he was able in a measure to attain his ends, in the face of gubernatorial opposition, and so too must be given credit for much that was done because it was at his advice that many projects were undertaken."

Reputation for Holiness

GENERALLY, the Church will not consider anyone for sainthood unless it can be proved that during his or her lifetime and ever since death the candidate enjoyed a reputation for holiness. The tradition of sanctity about Fray Junípero Serra can be traced back to his life-long companion and biographer, Fray Francisco Palou. On the frontispiece of his *Vida* is the inscription, He "died with a great reputation for holiness."

Antonio Furio's "The Martyrology for the Baleric Isles," printed at Palma de Mallorca in 1830, in treating of Serra, speaks of "the variety of virtues which adorned his soul in so eminent a degree, that both during his life and after his death, he was venerated as a saint."

During 1856, J.M. Rea Barcena wrote six articles about Serra, saying that the friar "died in the odor of sanctity for all who knew him and had associated with him." And the San Francisco *Call*, April 15, 1905, published an article about Serra which said that "some day doubtless Rome will see to it that the faithful missionary will be duly canonized."

Antonio Furio published his "Notes for the Church History of Mallorca," in 1820, and he notes of Father Serra that "he was zealous, chaste, humble, poor and obedient, having all these virtues equally in the highest degree. . . . (At his death) no words could express the grief of the Indians of that mission who called our venerable *Padre* a holy man, an angel sent by God for their relief."

In his *History of the Catholic Church in California*, (1871), Father William Gleeson wrote: "The very rare and extraordinary virtues practised by this remarkable man during the greater part of his life, made him be regarded by all as a person of the most eminent sanctity."

In the October, 1884, issue of *The Pilgrim of Palestine*, the Reverend Charles Vissani said "around the restored altar of San

Carlos . . . men of Spanish race and Indian, of Celtic and Saxon lineage, Italians, French and German, knelt offering the holy sacrifice as a propitiatory oblation in his behalf, while inwardly revering him and invoking his intercession."

Theodore Hittell, in his *History of California,* said that "Serra was very much such a man as St. Francis might have been, if he had lived in the 18th century." And Walter Smith, in *The Story of San Diego* (1892), said there was "one man whose name may yet find place in the roll of Catholic saints, Junípero Serra."

In 1900, Charles F. Carter wrote in his *Missions of Nueva California* that "surely (Serra) was one of the most remarkable men the Church has ever had, and one deserving canonization more than many others who have been so honored." In 1901, *The Tidings,* Catholic newspaper for the Diocese of Monterey-Los Angeles, quoted William E. Curtis as saying that Serra "was a very remarkable man, and I wonder that he has not yet been made a saint. His heroism, his usefulness, his self-sacrifice, his piety and his public services for the church and humanity certainly entitle him to canonization."

These are but a few of the litany of expressions about the uninterrupted tradition of holiness associated with Fray Junípero Serra.

Memorials to Serra

IN his monumental and classic life of Fray Junípero Serra, the late Maynard Geiger said that "in a sense Serra attained a certain immortality in memory. His fame has grown since his death, particularly since 1849. Monuments to him line his *Camino Real* from Petra to San Francisco."

Truly this humble Mallorcan friar who was so vital in life has projected his influence from the grave. His name has been bestowed upon buildings, ships, museums, highways, license plates and on and on.

The first public symbol of an appreciative posterity to Fray Junípero Serra was dedicated at Monterey, in 1891. Interestingly enough, the donor of this monument was Jane Leland Stanford, a non-Catholic. Located on a military reservation, it was unveiled on June 3, 1891, in the presence of over 5,000 people from every part of the west coast, many of whom arrived in specially chartered railroad cars.

The figure and pedestal are fashioned entirely of granite and the front faces almost due northeast. On a polished surface of the pedestal is an inscription which notes that "here, June 3, 1770, landed Very Rev. Father Junípero Serra, O.S.F. . . ."

In the nearby yard of San Carlos Cathedral, a stone marker in front of a gnarled old stump attests to a once-majestic tree which sheltered Fray Junípero as he offered the Liturgy inaugurating present-day Monterey. That almost-forgotten relic from an earlier age is, in reality, one of the oldest and most important historical mementos in the Western United States. Though now scarred and sadly-neglected, this bit of wood remnant, held together with chicken wire and concrete, has been associated with the area since the first white explorers entered Monterey Bay.

The picturesque statue of Fray Junípero Serra in San Francisco's Golden Gate Park depicts the Franciscan *Presidente* as the virile and vibrant personage he most assuredly was. The work of a local artist, it was unveiled in 1907.

Early that same year, Lilly Reichling Dyer, founder of the Native Daughters of the Golden West, launched a campaign throughout the state to have one of California's mountains named for Junípero Serra. Chosen for that distinction was the highest peak of the Santa Lucia mountains, a majestic eminence within view of the picturesque San Antonio de Padua Mission.

The designation of the peak as "Mount Junípero Serra" was officially announced at Washington, D.C., in mid-summer of 1907. News was released to Californians by *The Monitor* of San Francisco in its issue for August 17th.

These are only a smattering of the many memorials erected to the "Grey Ox." The works of Fray Junípero Serra, the standard-bearer of Christianity and the planter of European civilization in California, have been kept alive in the spoken and written word, in tradition, in books and in monuments across the lands of New Spain where the *Presidente* labored for thirty-five years.

With the coming of a new race and a new flag, with fresh political ideas and frequently differing religious beliefs, with men bent on adventure and the acquisition of wealth, one might surmise that the name of Serra would be relegated to an innocuous place in the dead past. Precisely the opposite is the case!

Remembrances of the Presidente

IN a recent newspaper poll, three hundred Californians were asked to identify "the most important person in the state's history." Interestingly, 64% nominated a Franciscan friar who died in 1784. The name and accomplishments of Fray Junípero Serra are very much alive to contemporary peoples. Nowhere is that more obvious than in the Serra nomenclature one finds around the state.

There is the Junípero Serra Museum (San Diego), the Serra State Building (Los Angeles), the Serra Hotel (Monterey) and the Serra Memorial Hospital (Los Angeles).

And then there are dozens of streets named after the friar, including Serra Street (San Buenaventura), *Avenida* Junípero (San Clemente), Junípero Street (San Gabriel), *Alameda Padre Serra* (Santa Barbara), Serra Drive (Atascadero) and the Serra Highway (101).

In addition, there was a Liberty ship (S.S. Junípero Serra), a railroad station (Santa Fe, San Juan Capistrano), a Boys Club (Los Angeles), a camp (Angeles National Forest), a public school (San Francisco) and a retreat house (Malibu). There's even a "SERRA" license plate adorning the car driven by Father Noel Moholy, the Vice Postulator for the Serra Cause. Among the organizations bearing the friar's name, the largest is Serra International which was founded on February 27, 1935, in Seattle, Washington. Fittingly, this group of dedicated people concentrate their efforts towards vocations to the ministry.

Among others claiming or invoking the name are the Serra Council of Catholic Foresters, the Court of Junípero Serra (Catholic Daughters), Junípero Serra Council No. 14 (Young Mens Institute) and Serra General Assembly (Fourth Degree, Knights of Columbus, Oakland). Oldest of these groups would probably date from 1903, when the Native Daughters of the

Golden West instituted a parlor in Monterey which has since been known as Junípero Parlor No. 141.

Earliest among the public proclamations honoring the Mallorcan priest was issued on November 24, 1913, when Governor Hiram Johnson officially proclaimed the 200th anniversary of Serra's birth a legal holiday in California. Serra's name and/or figure has philatelic significance too. It has appeared on at least five stamps from Portugal, Mexico and Spain. Hopefully the United States will soon follow suit.

There are several Serra windows, including one at Dolores Mission Basilica (San Francisco) which mistakenly has the friar outfitted in a brown habit. There are others at San Diego (Immaculate Conception), Camarillo (Saint Mary Magdalen) and San Francisco (Saint Mary). Holy Name College in Washington, D.C., contains a bust of Serra on its ornate facade.

Richard Keys Biggs and Arthur Bienbar composed Masses dedicated to Fray Junípero Serra. Jose Mojica wrote a song which he entitled "*Padre de California,*" and a special march was composed in honor of Serra by the Mallorcan band leader Moya, in 1913. Among the dramas, pageants, poems and articles about Serra, the most successful was that written by John Steven McGroarty. "The Mission Play" was performed before hundreds of thousands from all over the world at San Gabriel.

On and on the list could go. For Californians, Fray Junípero Serra and what he embodied are an important part of their heritage. Their prayer is that the Holy Father will soon proclaim this great and holy servant of God among the Church's *beati.*

Spiritual Father for California

WITH prophetic insight, John F. Davis wrote, in 1913, that the pathetic ruin at Carmel "is a shattered monument above a grave that will become a world's shrine of pilgrimage in honor of one of humanity's heroes." He went on to say of Fray Junípero Serra that "the memory of the brave heart that was here consumed with love for mankind will live through the ages. And, in a sense, the work of these missions is not dead—their very ruins still preach the lesson of service and of sacrifice."

The dedicated missionary who is regarded by all peoples as the spiritual father of Alta California was a man of outstanding personal qualities. The testimony of his contemporaries and subsequent commentators are unanimous in their praise of the Mallorcan friar.

Serra's apostolic philosophy was stated in a letter he wrote to his superior, shortly after arriving at San Diego. "It will be necessary in the beginning to suffer many real privations. However, to a lover all things are sweet." Serra expected no Utopia. He presupposed hardships and even embraced them. He took setbacks and disappointments in stride.

The friar was made of tough spiritual fibre. For years he was accustomed to four or five hours of sleep only. He spent long hours in prayer. In the matter of food, he was most abstemious and seemed to care little about its quality. He had prepared himself well for the rigorous apostolate of a cheerless frontier.

A measure of the esteem generally held for Fray Junípero Serra by his contemporaries is evident from a confrere who write to a friend, on August 26, 1773: "Because of the austerity of his life, his humility, charity and other virtues, he is worthy to be counted among the imitators of the apostles."

Like all truly spiritual people, Serra spoke rarely and with great reservations about his own interior life. The friar did pull aside the curtain long enough to observe that "the only quality that I can feel pretty sure I have, by the kindness and grace of God, is my good intentions. As to anything else, what means have I of knowing whether I am right or wrong? May God direct us in the way of truth!

Isidore Dockweiler said that "this man whose memory is indissolubly one with the epic of California, was great in humility. He triumphed by his courage, when everything would have appeared bound to discourage him and beat him down. He is one who is worthy of first place among the immortal heroes who created our nation. So his memory will never die, and his name will be blessed from generation to generation."

Over half a century ago, Hiram Johnson, California's outstanding senator and governor, made bold to say:

To the memory of Junípero Serra, California owes an everlasting tribute. He brought civilization to our land, and in deed and character, he deserves a foremost place in the history of our state.

And surely that he has attained!

Candidate for Sainthood

SAINTS differ from one to another, just as human character varies from brother to sister. Grace enhances and ennobles nature. So in each saint, one beholds natural basic character elevated by grace. A person's position in life does much to determine the emphasis on particular virtues. A missionary on a barbarous frontier, introducing Christianity to an alien civilization, will not be remembered for practicing the identical virtues exemplified in the life of a cloistered Carmelite nun in faraway Spain.

Fray Junípero Serra worked out his salvation under a bureaucratic government, where the state ruled the Church in most external matters. He had to function in an uncultured society, but this he did by choice.

Half of Serra's adult life were spent in educational work. He was a professor of theology subject to ecclesial, civil and military control who somehow managed to succeed on the frontier.

Serra was and remains a public figure. He had to deal with illiterate Indians and rough soldiers, yet he was able to win the attention of governors, viceroys and kings. So forceful was his impact that today his image stands on the grounds of the state capitol at Sacramento and in Statuary Hall in Washington, D.C.

External prominence however, is not sufficient grounds for beatification. It merely portrays Serra as an eminent personage with a successful career. Candidates for sainthood must practice, to an heroic degree, the virtues of faith, hope, charity and humility, as well as the cardinal virtues of prudence, justice, temperance and fortitude.

Serra's written words and personal actions had to be scrutinized and appraised in view of his particular vocation as priest, religious, evangelizer and government servant. Fortunately, the friar's life is an open book. It is precisely because so much is known about him that so much had to be considered.

When Serra's biographer wrote and published the first life of the friar, he added to it a schema of his virtues, evidently believing that one day Serra might be considered for sainthood. Though well-written, the testimony of one man, who knew Serra for over forty years, was insufficient. The views of others needed to be considered.

Actually, much of the evidence subsequently gathered outshines the account of Fray Francisco Palou. One person, for example, had written to Spain that "all said openly that the man was a saint, and that his actions were those of an apostle."

The monumental testimony presented to the Sacred Congregation for Saints in the 620 page *Summarium* and its lengthy supplementary volume indicates that in life, at death and ever since there has been an unending chorus of encomiums concerning Fray Junípero Serra's worthiness for beatification.

The late Father Maynard Geiger once wrote that "Serra is on trial. His own doctoral examination in Palma was a picnic compared to this. Finally all roads lead to Rome. Serra made many voyages and journeys and he may find his journey to Rome the longest, the most difficult and fatiguing of them all."

Of course, Serra will always be the Serra of the history books and the Serra of the household phrase. But once he is given the honor of the altar, he would be officially called "Blessed" and later "Saint" Junípero.

A California Saint—?

CANONIZATION, or the formal declaration by the Catholic Church of a particular individual's personal salvation, has always been described as "the most complicated legal process in the world." Such a proclamation usually marks the end of centuries of research, discussion and purposeful delay.

In 1909, Charles Fletcher Lummis, the prominent historian and non-Catholic founder of the Southwest Museum, noted that "without authority, I have started a campaign to find out why JUNIPERO SERRA has not been canonized." Though Lummis never published the results of his searching, the answer to the original query was given years later by Serra's official biographer.

The principal unfavorable factors against the opening of a cause of sainthood in favor of Serra in colonial California were distance, the absence of a bishop, a lack of personnel, great expense and the changing political situation not too long after Serra's death.

However, the question became so compelling that in 1934 the name of Fray Junípero Serra was formally proposed for the honors of the altar by the Very Reverend Novatus Bensing, Provincial of the Franciscan Province of Santa Barbara. An historical commission was established by the Bishop of Monterey-Fresno on December 17, 1943. Three well-known scholars, one of them a non-Catholic were instructed to collect all existing writings of Serra and all data concerning his life, character and reputation. The work of finding, gathering and assembling the necessary materials from over 125 libraries and archives from around the world took five years of dedicated effort on the part of Father Maynard J. Geiger, O.F.M.

People of Mexican, Spanish, Indian and early American ancestry were interviewed on what they knew of Father Serra from family tradition. Out of this testimony, the vice-postulator drew up a series of statements to be proven in an ecclesial forum.

Formal court proceedings began on December 12, 1948 at Fresno, presided over by Bishop Aloysius J. Willinger. Oaths of fidelity and secrecy were taken by all attached to the cause. Specially chosen judges were empowered to interrogate witnesses with questions submitted by the Promoter of the Faith, or the "Devil's Advocate." At this hearing the 2420 documents (7500 pages) of Serra's writings were carefully examined for doctrinal content.

All sessions were held behind locked doors to prevent any possible collusion. The vice-postulator, after an initial appearance, took no part in the investigation process, "the only court in the world in which the man who is pleading the case is not allowed to be present!" After four days at Fresno, the court reconvened at Carmel, burial place of Junípero Serra. There another process was inaugurated to ascertain whether any unauthorized veneration had taken place. The judges, seated in the sanctuary, questioned a number of early pioneers "as to the nature of the pilgrimages and devotions in honor of *Padre* Serra after his death in 1784."

Subsequently, testimony was given by members of the Diocesan Historical Commission concerning the 5000 pages of materials written *about* Serra by kings, viceroys, clergymen, military people, civilians and confreres. At the conclusion of these and later court sessions, reports of the meetings were packed in boxes, stamped with the episcopal seal, and shipped to Rome's Sacred Congregation of Rites for further examination.

The recent publication of the *Summarium* and its lengthy supplementary volume of Serra's worthiness for beatification complete the canonical process. Fray Junípero Serra needs only the formal approval and declaration of the Holy Father before taking his place among those known in Christian annals as the "sanctified of the Lord."

California
Two Centuries Later

THE 200th anniversary of Fray Junípero Serra's demise is an appropriate occasion for reflecting on the mustard seed planted by the Mallorcan friar and his priestly collaborators along California's *El Camino Real*. Early visionaries like Harrison Gray Otis, editor of the Los Angeles *Times*, foresaw the growth potential of California even before the turn of the present century.

Others, more spiritually inclined, looked at the state's majestic mountains, deserts and the placid blue Pacific and almost instinctively sensed, as Aimee Semple McPherson told her followers, that in California one could find "God's great blueprint for man's abode on earth."

In the decade of the 1980s, such visions have all but come true. California has become the promised land of the New World. Large masses of people have opted to leave behind the bitter cold of winter, to abandon the crime, dirt, noise and diminished prospects of the older half of America for California, the nation-state of the emergent sunbelt, the place where the rainbow ends.

Were Francisco Palou to update his life of Fray Junípero Serra, he would surely observe that today there are at least five and maybe even a dozen Californias. There is the barren splendor of the desert lands to the south and the magnificent scenery of the mountains and forests in the north. There are the 500 stupendous miles of Sierras and the crop-rich farmland of the vast central valley.

Future historians will record that 200 years after Fray Junípero Serra had fallen asleep in the Lord, his California had become not alone the top agricultural state in America, but its leading industrial power as well. By 1978, the state boasted the nation's largest commercial bank, the top six savings and loan companies, the biggest retail food chain, the largest construction engineering firm and the leading producers of both gold and television films.

In imitation of the Mallorcan friar who began it all, Californians of modern times have been characteristically more willing than others to experiment and break with tradition. It was precisely their willingness to try difficult things, to look at sagebrush and mesquite and see farms and cities, which has pushed California to its present position of national dominance.

Serra and the host of others who built California were not traditionalists. They used, for example, new strains of crops that could be grown in the dry soil, they dug wells and fashioned canals to nourish and bring alive the barren ground. They believed that under God technology and innovation could solve any problem and that conviction was the key to California's breathtaking rise to economic prominence in the past century.

On and on the statisticians could go. The story of the California bequeathed by Fray Junípero Serra to succeeding generations is certainly among the most remarkable in all of recorded history. And how would Serra react at seeing his vineyard as America's number one center of religious, political, economical and social power? Likely he would simply smile and repeat once again: "In California is my life and there, God willing, I hope to die."

The Serra Beatification

ETCHED deeply onto the marble face-stone of a papal tomb in Saint Peter's Basilica is an inscription which says that "the faith of the Church is anchored to it s history." Surely that truism described the scene that took place there on September 25th, 1988, when Pope John Paul II formally beatified Fray Junípero Serra.

What a thrilling and rewarding experience it was to hear the Vicar of Christ venerating and extolling the memory of the humble Mallorcan friar who introduced the saving message of Christianity to the western shores of America.

It was a distinction that the friar would have preferred to share with Juan Crespi (his student), Francisco Palou (his biographer), Fermin Lasuen (his successor) and all the other Franciscans who ministered along Alta California's *El Camino Real*.

Surely there was a chorus of affirmation to the Holy Father's proclamation—from Juan Perez who found a watery grave in the Pacific, from Felipe de Neve who succumbed in the Sonoran desert, from Antonio Bucareli who is buried in the old Basilica of Our Lady of Guadalupe, from Teodore de Croix who died as Viceroy of Peru and from Rafael Verger who completed his life as Bishop of Nuevo Leon.

For a few brief moments, the pageantry of California's colonization was restaged, this time before the largest audience ever. It was easy to visualize the shadowy figures of Jose de Galvez, Fernando Rivera and even Pedro Fages solemnly escorting the limping, gray-robed friar to the chair of Peter's successor.

And, off to the side, one could faintly make out the choir of young voices that Serra trained to chant the Mass and Divine Office at San Carlos Borromeo Mission. They were there to represent the thousands of native Americans who benefitted from Serra's ministry and that of his companions.

The whole event was considerably more than a routine liturgical occurrence. It was a day of fulfillment for such personages as Joachim Adam, Zephyrin Engelhardt, Herbert Eugene Bolton, Harry Downie, Maynard Geiger and the host of others who kept alive the memory of Serra for this and future generations.

And there were "real" people there too—people of the 1980s whose lives have been touched by Fray Junípero Serra. California's cardinal, one of its archbishops, numerous bishops, clergy and religious were there, as were representatives from all Serra's nine missions in Alta California, his foundations in the Serra Gorda region of Mexico and his homeland of Mallorca. And how rightfully proud was the mayor of the tiny village of Petra, Serra's birthplace, to see a native son so singularly honored.

As the Holy Father slowly read out the formula entrolling Fray Junípero Serra among the Church's *beati,* one couldn't help recalling the prophetic nature of the circular letter dispatched from Mexico City announcing the friar's earthly demise in 1784.

Therein Juan Sancho de la Torre became the first to suggest what Pope John Paul II confirmed for all the world to hear, 204 years later, that Serra was indeed a person who practiced heroic virtue. Sancho put it this way: "So great was his charity which he always manifested toward those poor Indians that not only the ordinary people, but likewise persons of higher condition were struck with admiration.

"All people said openly that that man was a saint and that his actions were those of an apostle. This has been the opinion concerning him every since he arrived in this kingdom. This opinion has been constant and without interruption."